HOOKED
ON
ENGLISH!

*Ready-to-Use Activities
for the English Curriculum,
Grades 7-12*

JACK UMSTATTER

JOSSEY-BASS
A Wiley Imprint
www.josseybass.com

Published by Jossey-Bass
A Wiley Imprint
989 Market Street, San Francisco, CA 94103-1741   www.josseybass.com

Jossey-Bass books and products are available through most bookstores. To contact Jossey-Bass directly
call our Customer Care Department within the U.S. at 800-956-7739, outside the U.S. at 317-572-3986
or fax 317-572-4002.

Jossey-Bass also publishes its books in a variety of electronic formats. Some content that appears in
print may not be available in electronic books.

Library of Congress Cataloging-in-Publication Data
Umstatter, Jack
      Hooked on English! : ready-to-use activities for the English
curriculum, grades 7-12 / Jack Umstatter.
        p.   cm.
      ISBN 0-87628-421-7
      ISBN 0-7879-6584-7 (layflat)
      1. English language—Study and teaching (Secondary)   2. Education,
Secondary—Activity programs.   I. Title.
LB1631.U48   1997
428'.0071'2—dc21   97-19772

FIRST EDITION
HB Printing 10 9 8 7 6 5 4 3 2

DEDICATION

Again for Chris, Kate, and Maureen

ACKNOWLEDGMENTS

My thanks to Win Huppuch and Connie Kallback for their skill and continued support.

To my students for their enthusiasm.

Special thanks to Dover Publications for the use of illustrations from the Dover Clip Art Series.

To Terry from WISCO COMPUTING of Wisconsin Rapids, Wisconsin 54495 for his programs.

Martin Luther King's Speech in Section Five was prepared by Gerald Murphy (The Cleveland Free-Net—aa300) and distributed by the Cybercasting Services Division of the National Public Telecomputing Network (NPTN).

Definitions for certain words are taken from *Webster's New World Dictionary, Third College Edition*, 1988 published by Simon & Schuster, Inc.

ABOUT THE AUTHOR

Jack Umstatter has taught English and literature on both the junior high and senior high school levels since 1972, and education and literature at Dowling College in Oakdale, New York, for the past six years. He currently teaches English in the Cold Spring Harbor School District in New York.

Mr. Umstatter graduated from Manhattan College with a B.A. in English and completed his M.A. in English at S.U.N.Y.-Stony Brook. He earned his Educational Administration degree at Long Island University.

Mr. Umstatter has been selected Teacher of the Year several times and most recently was elected to *Who's Who Among America's Teachers*. He has taught all levels of secondary English classes including the Honors and Advanced Placement classes. As coach of the high school's 1991 Academic Team, the Brainstormers, he led the team in capturing the Long Island and New York State championships when competing in the American Scholastic Competition Network National Tournament of Champions in Lake Forest, Illinois.

Mr. Umstatter's other publications include *Hooked On Literature!*, *201 Ready-to-Use Word Games for the English Classroom*, and *Brain Games!* all published by The Center for Applied Research in Education.

ABOUT THIS RESOURCE

Just a reminder—lesson plans are due tomorrow. Faculty meeting is next week. That stack of essays in your briefcase is not getting any smaller. It might even be thicker than the stack on your desk. Did you get to prepare that novel unit yet? Have those grammar quizzes been graded? When are those short story tests going to be corrected? Tomorrow and tomorrow and tomorrow...

To do or not to do? There is no question! It has to get done! Few envy the amount of work (and hours) expected of you. Fewer would be able to summon the energy, discipline, and creativity to get through it.

Hooked On English! was designed with you, the busy English teacher, in mind. Organized into seven sections that cover many different English topics from grammar to composition, this book is an easy-to-use resource loaded with over 185 fun-filled, creative, and practical ready-to-use reproducible activities that will stimulate your students to think and enjoy learning in your English classroom. These stimulating classroom-tested exercises have received very positive student responses and have resulted in a greater understanding and appreciation of the material. For your convenience, the Table of Contents provided a quick and useful guide to locating the desired activity. To save you additional valuable time, answer keys accompany the activities. Some of the activities use magic squares, riddles, hidden words and sayings, word finds and other devices that allow students to check their own answers.

Mention the topics grammar, usage, vocabulary, or mechanics in class tomorrow and your students might roll their eyes, bite their tongues, or ask for a pass to the nurse. The first four sections of *Hooked On English!* cover these four topics in a refreshingly entertaining and enjoyable way. Students will retain the material better and more eagerly. Section Five, "Composition," will stimulate your students to write more creatively and convincingly. Section Six, "Literature," includes practical activities that can be applied to the literature your class is reading. The final section, "The Everyday Use of Our Language," ties the other sections together as the students see their language brought to life in the media and other informational sources.

Through reproducible activities including crossword puzzles, jumbles, word finds, magic squares, cryptoquotes, matchings, fill-ins, word scrambles, and more, *Hooked on English!* provides your students with exciting ways to learn and enjoy English. It offers you the opportunity to use the activities for homework, tests, quizzes, research, extra credit, discussions, bees, cooperative learning, and any other application you see fit to use.

In addition to the student activities, you'll find an extremely useful appendix entitled "The Internet Connection" that lists valuable sites with information on authors, education, grammar, language arts, lesson plans, literature, research, words and writing.

In short, this ready-to-use resource will allow you a few minutes to sit back and relax instead of doing additional work. You deserve it! Enjoy!

Jack Umstatter

CONTENTS

SECTION ONE: GRAMMAR (30)

SECTION TWO: USAGE (25)

SECTION THREE: VOCABULARY (32)

SECTION FOUR: MECHANICS AND WORDPLAY (24)

SECTION FIVE: COMPOSITION & PUBLIC SPEAKING (29)

SECTION SIX: LITERATURE (23)

SECTION SEVEN: THE EVERYDAY USE OF OUR LANGUAGE (23)

Answer Keys (201-279)

Section One

GRAMMAR

1. AND THE PART OF SPEECH IS...

There is a word missing in each sentence below. Fill in the space with a word of your choice and then in the space following the sentence, identify that word's part of speech.

1. The elderly man walked _____ into the room. _____

2. None _____ the ladies requested anything else. _____

3. Fourteen _____ animals were flown to the distant zoo. _____

4. Kyle _____ help with the plans for the Denver trip. _____

5. The workers will neither strike _____ picket because of the low wages.
   _____

6. _____ the next few months, we will prepare our move to England.
   _____

7. _____! I never thought we would win the lottery. _____

8. A missing _____ was found on the subway. _____

9. The referee's whistle was _____ on the floor as she ran down the court.
   _____

10. A bag of popcorn _____ a jar of mayonnaise were left on the store shelf.
    _____

11. The car's _____ were buried in the snow. _____

12. Silenced by the crowd, the speaker _____ the rally was humiliated.
    _____

2. FUN WITH PARTS OF SPEECH

The word **down** can be used as five different parts of speech. Yet, if we told you which five, you would have the first five answers to this activity. You wouldn't want that, would you? Write the underlined word's part of speech in the space following each sentence. A score of 17 or better is to be commended. Good luck!

1. The <u>down</u> jacket was purchased here. _____

2. <u>Down</u> the ball on the ten yard line. _____

3. Look <u>down</u> the hall to see if he is there. _____

4. Patsy fell <u>down</u> after James pushed her. _____

5. The Chargers made the first <u>down</u>. _____

6. Do you like the <u>snow</u>? _____

7. I think it will <u>snow</u> tonight. _____

8. Please don't <u>light</u> the cigarette in this room. _____

9. A <u>light</u> rain was falling over the fields. _____

10. The traffic <u>light</u> was broken. _____

11. He wanted to travel <u>light</u>. _____

12. The <u>past</u> is fondly remembered by the team. _____

13. We studied the <u>past</u> tense of the verb. _____

14. He walked slowly <u>past</u> us. _____

15. They drove <u>beyond</u> the huge mountain. _____

16. We spoke about the great <u>beyond</u>. _____

17. The <u>part</u> in her hair was quite straight. _____

18. Unfortunately, we must <u>part</u> now. _____

19. What's your <u>take</u> on the whole thing? _____

20. <u>Take</u> a piece of advice from me. _____

3. SPREADING THE WEALTH

All eight parts of speech are treated fairly here since there are three examples of each in this activity. Above each underlined word indicate its part of speech by using the following abbreviations: noun (n), pronoun (p), verb (v), adjective (adj), adverb (advb), conjunction (c), preposition (prep), and interjection (i).

1. <u>None</u> of the players <u>is</u> going <u>to</u> the assembly.

2. We will <u>immediately</u> go there <u>and</u> see your <u>project</u>.

3. Let us remember the story about the <u>needy</u> people <u>who</u> live near the river.

4. <u>Ugh!</u> This mess <u>demands</u> immediate attention.

5. I'll have either lasagna <u>or</u> roast beef.

6. Ursula <u>gracefully</u> entered the <u>crowded</u> room <u>because</u> she knew <u>people</u> would be watching her.

7. <u>Wow!</u> In three more days the program will be broadcast to over seventy countries.

8. Mike and George left their <u>gloves</u> <u>at</u> the movies.

9. Please bring the package to <u>us</u> <u>now</u>.

10. <u>Ouch!</u> The musician <u>walked</u> <u>into</u> the <u>cement</u> wall and hurt her hand.

4. COMMON NOUNS ARE WHAT WE WANT!

After you have underlined every common noun, write each one's first letter on the line below the last question. When written in this consecutive order, the letters form a famous quotation by poet John Donne. Write the quotation in the appropriate space below.

1. The lost necklace was found in the overcoat.

2. We heard that the magician made his announcement on the news.

3. The implications are not really the solutions.

4. An army takes no nonsense from these inhabitants.

5. A specialist in the laws of alimony usually does well in negotiations.

6. The experienced dentist still had great enthusiasm for naming the old teams.

7. Indecisiveness is a reality.

8. No eulogist draws his listeners in by yelling.

9. The opportunity to buy inexpensive furniture now should be an inducement.

10. Our favorite teacher had her students review the economy.

11. The love of our friends can be very important to us.

The letters are: _____

The John Donne quotation is: _____

5. IS THOMAS EDISON A PROPER OR COMMON ONE?

Proper? Common? Of course, we mean a proper or common noun and Thomas Edison is a proper noun. Inventor is the common noun that we associate with Thomas Edison. In this activity you will match the proper nouns in Column A with their common nouns in Column B. Each answer is used only once. If you have correctly written the answers, you will find three types of fish in the answer column. Write their names in the sentence following the last question.

Column A		Column B	
1. _____ Beatles		a.	psychoanalyst
2. _____ Canada		b.	patriot
3. _____ Mariah Carey		c.	actor
4. _____ Jim Carrey		d.	explorer
5. _____ Cheers		e.	dramatist
6. _____ Columbus		f.	author
7. _____ Descartes		g.	city
8. _____ Charles Dickens		h.	printer
9. _____ Emily Dickinson		i.	planet
10. _____ Dumb and Dumber		j.	organization
11. _____ Thomas Edison		k.	cartoonist
12. _____ French		l.	musical group
13. _____ Freud		m.	god
14. _____ Girl Scouts		n.	language
15. _____ Patrick Henry		o.	television program
16. _____ Indianapolis		p.	president
17. _____ Michael Jordan		q.	athlete
18. _____ North Dakota		r.	country
19. _____ Theodore Roosevelt		s.	singer
20. _____ Saturn		t.	movie
21. _____ Charles Schultz		u.	inventor
22. _____ William Shakespeare		v.	poet
23. _____ John Philip Sousa		w.	mathematician
24. _____ John Peter Zenger		x.	state
25. _____ Zeus		y.	composer

The three types of fish found in the answer column are _____,
_____ and _____.

Name _____ Date _____ Period _____

6. A NOUN AND ITS USES

This activity features the noun in six of its uses. The noun is used as a subject (s.), an object (o.), an object of the preposition (o.p.), an indirect object (i.o.), a predicate noun (p.n.), and an appositive (app.). Each is used three times. On the line after each sentence, write the correct abbreviation to show the underlined noun's use in that sentence.

1. She is his new <u>girlfriend</u>. _____

2. He released the <u>doves</u> from the cage. _____

3. I gave the <u>boss</u> no reason to complain. _____

4. The <u>weather</u> has not been too favorable lately. _____

5. They received the <u>applause</u> of the crowd. _____

6. Lyndon B. Johnson, the former <u>president</u>, was a Democrat. _____

7. Some of the people do not care to walk in the <u>parade</u>. _____

8. James P. Murphy is a <u>scholar</u>. _____

9. The new <u>toaster</u> was purchased as a gift. _____

10. Texas, the <u>Lone Star State</u>, is quite large. _____

11. His reasons for not joining are not sufficient for our <u>approval</u>. _____

12. Both referees told <u>Mike</u> that he had to tuck in his jersey. _____

13. We gave the lonely <u>cat</u> some fresh milk. _____

14. Throw the <u>ball</u> to me. _____

15. Joe Smith, the <u>director</u>, will now answer the question. _____

16. Walk slowly across this <u>beam</u>. _____

17. <u>Mathematics</u> is a very interesting subject. _____

18. Lucille Ball was a <u>comedienne</u>. _____

7. NINES ARE EVERYWHERE

All fifteen sentences have pronouns in them. If you correctly identify the pronouns in each line and add up the number of letters in the pronouns, the total number of letters per line should be nine. Circle your pronouns and start counting!

1. All of them are sitting near me.

2. One is helping us to move them.

3. He and she can remember some of the names.

4. Those are many of the correct answers.

5. Nobody told her the restaurant's address.

6. Each of the girls remembered many of the names I had earlier recalled.

7. This is yours.

8. Who wants to purchase any of the cards designed by him?

9. Helen, who enjoys reading mystery novels, recommended some to us.

10. "Anybody can solve it," said the police chief to the newspaper reporters.

11. Either you or they can help me do the job a little better.

12. The word Kellie wants to explain more thoroughly is the word ourselves.

13. What is the reason I should give to them?

14. Unlike me, Mike wants to drive by himself.

15. I can do much of that.

8. THESE INDEFINITE PRONOUNS ARE DEFINITELY HIDDEN!

Indefinite pronouns do not refer to a definite person or thing and are frequently used without antecedents. A word such as **both** in the sentence, "**Both** are intelligent," is an example of an indefinite pronoun since it takes the place of a noun (two in this instance), does not refer to a specific person or thing, and has no antecedent or word it refers to in the sentence.

Listed below the puzzle are the twenty-five indefinite pronouns we've hidden. Words are placed backwards, forward, diagonally, up and down. Find and circle them.

```
P C N H F P V M S H V L Z X T B P G C C K T V L
F J D W B F M Q P V Z H Z T W V Y B C K N R W Z
R Y F J T N Q P D E G T E X Q M Q M K M Y M S J
K P M P N L D M R V J V L A O T X T R A Q A V P
L B M L R Y T G O F E V Q S N W Y F V N N Z H S
H A G N E I T H E R E H T O N Y D O B Y N A V S
F P R G B H H J Y Y E V R R D D T H D N P O T N
F L F E E Q T O G T K F T O Y O S H X J B S N D
E M O S V A N O T H E R B F R B J O I A L L M E
W A R Y E E N Q B I R O H Z G E K M M N D T U B
R D C T R E S C G N N X X P X M H L L E G M C B
V R N H Y F R D M G V V G Y V O D T S Y O R H D
K B K F B F X F Q D R R T S D S Z H I C H N B Z
C C G G O Q P N N B M G F N F R K H F E N W E N
H Y G F D D L C Y M D P Q W X Y S G P P B D V T
B B W N Y C P C Q S Y P J S N M X F Z P F G N P
L Z V P V V J K N B J C K X H N T Z K B F T V Y
```

ALL	EITHER	MOST	SEVERAL
ANOTHER	EVERYBODY	MUCH	SOME
ANY	EVERYONE	NEITHER	SOMEBODY
ANYBODY	EVERYTHING	NOBODY	SOMEONE
ANYTHING	FEW	NONE	
BOTH	MANY	ONE	
EACH	MORE	OTHER	

9. FINDING FIVE VERBS

If you can identify the prepositional phrases in the following sentences, you are on your way to finding five verbs. Underline the prepositional phrases in the sentences and then circle the first letter of the preposition. Write these letters consecutively on the line beneath the last sentence and you can spell out the five verbs formed by those letters.

1. By Thursday we will be on the plane over Los Angeles.

2. Tony listened to the complaints during the raucous meeting.

3. The names of students without lunch passes are here.

4. Near my locker before lunch, we talked about the problems in Bosnia.

5. The sun was moving toward the horizon.

6. He is like his brother.

7. Joe jumped on the bandwagon.

8. The director walked around the set during the rehearsals.

9. We are near the taxi station.

10. Around this league, you are the finest gymnast.

11. The artist reached inside his pocket like this.

The first letters of the prepositions are: _____

_____.

The words the letters spell out are: _____, _____,

_____, _____, and _____.

10. ONLY CERTAIN LETTERS COUNT HERE!

Underline the main verb in each sentence. In Group A, write the **first** and **third** letters of the verb on the line below sentence five. Unscramble the letters to identify a word that is the name of both a famous person and a famous place. In Group B, circle the first **two** letters of each verb and write the letters on the line below sentence ten. Unscramble the letters to identify a famous American city.

Group A

1. He schemed his way to the top.

2. Are they gathering the leaves near the road?

3. The climbers were weaving their way through the woods.

4. The wealthy family also owns the house by the lake.

5. Can you innovate another method?

The letters are: _____

The famous person and place is _____.

Group B

6. The woman, known for her memory, identified the missing person.

7. Seeing the family's need, the workers provided the necessary help.

8. Will they overcome the tremendous odds against them?

9. Celebrate the victory now!

10. Thrilled with their accomplishments, they enjoyed themselves immensely.

The letters are: _____

The famous American city is _____.

11. LOOKING FOR THOSE ADJECTIVES

Forty-five adjectives are waiting for you to find them in this puzzle. The adjectives, listed below, are placed backwards, forward, diagonally, and up and down. Good luck!

```
S R L T L P P J M T A Y S D C V N Q D Y J V A C
A G F T S N R R M P S V K R H X G V E R B G B S
I C L H Z F W A A S T N E D X L N C S V I T R N
M Z C O L B A T H C U A Z V J A O D S L B A I F
P O P U L A R T I S T I C S K I L L E D E L G L
O S E G R U M A N I E I Z T M C U U L R V L H Z
R N B H S A P W V E N L C D Z E F F B I I E T L
T B Q T L K T E L E D P O A M P D I A N T M S T
A K E F O C I E D L E I R V L S N T P T P O D F
N D M U Y L L N I B R F F U E L I U A E E S E A
T C F L A K A H D A E A R N D L M A C L C D L M
N H A E L B U A N T L H L A O E Y E G L R N I S
A B G R K Z T P E O E E M U G C N B T I E A C Y
I Q C U E D C P L N G A W T C R P T D G P H I P
L G W C F F N Y P Y A R P J V S A Y T E W D O J
A K S E W D U J S R N T M M V B U N F N V N U F
V Y G S Q J P L F F T Y P N D K L M T T X F S N
```

ACCURATE
ADMIRED
AGILE
ARTISTIC
ASTUTE
BEAUTIFUL
BLESSED
BRAVE
BRIGHT
CAPABLE
CAREFUL
CONFIDENT

CREATIVE
DELICIOUS
ELEGANT
FLUENT
FRAGRANT
HANDSOME
HAPPY
HEARTY
IMPORTANT
INTELLIGENT
KIND
LONG

LOVELY
LOYAL
MINDFUL
MUSCULAR
NOTABLE
PERCEPTIVE
POPULAR
PRACTICAL
PRUDENT
PUNCTUAL
SECURE
SHARP

SKILLED
SPECIAL
SPLENDID
TALL
TENDER
THOUGHTFUL
TRUSTED
VALIANT
WARM

12. ANIMALS AND ADVERBS

Twenty-three adverbs are found within these sentences. Underline the adverb and then write its first letter in the space below the last question. Unscramble these letters to find the names of five animals.

1. He gladly returned the missing items.

2. Evidently the young players often try to imitate the professionals.

3. We recently memorized the newly designed arrangement of teams.

4. Doug was not immediately flustered by the extremely difficult test.

5. He approached the assignment there both slowly and carefully.

6. Later we will kindly help you.

7. They want to travel more rapidly.

8. The singer only wanted the audience to enjoy the performance.

9. It's too early to know completely.

10. Lori did her work intelligently and accurately.

11. They openly discussed the problems.

12. He acted youthfully.

The letters are: _____

The five animals are _____, _____,

_____, _____, and _____.

13. PREPOSITIONS AND DRINKS

If you correctly circle the first letter of each consecutive preposition, you will spell out four drinks. Write the letters on the line below the last question and then write the six drinks on the line after that one.

1. Luke went through all the books except this one.

2. He walked his sister across the stream.

3. The discussion concerning politics was broadcast over several radio stations.

4. He was much like you at that age.

5. Since your meeting, he looked over the report during his free time at work.

6. Within the next six months, he will look into the tragic situation.

7. The cat feels comfortable near everyone except Ted.

8. Martin climbed to the top of the mountain near Harrisville.

9. Many students in junior high school enjoy conversations concerning their rights.

10. Within two months, he will travel across the country toward California.

11. Josie likes all her classes except math.

12. His speech regarding the erosion problem was fascinating.

The letters are: _____

The four drinks are _____, _____,

_____, and _____.

© 1998 by John Wiley & Sons, Inc

14. OVER THE RIVER AND THROUGH THE WOODS TO GRANDMOTHER'S HOUSE WE GO!

This long title includes three prepositional phrases to alert you that the prepositional phrases are on their way in this activity. Underline the twenty prepositional phrases in the next paragraph. Then write the first letter of each prepositional phrase on the appropriate line found after the paragraph. If done correctly, you will spell out in consecutive order a famous place along the Hudson River in New York, something your body needs, and a famous trio. Good luck!

Manny can't seem to live without exercise. Every day except Sundays he lifts weights and runs. Since 1995 he has worked toward his goal. He went past his original goal. Over the summer he will run in the long race held near Toronto, Canada. Throughout the spring he never wavered from his workout routine. Like his older sister, Manny will exercise under any weather conditions — hot or cold. In many circumstances he felt fatigue during his training. About three weeks ago Manny ran the fifteen-mile race by himself since his training partner was away. Any questions Manny had concerning his fitness level were answered that day.

The first letters of each preposition (in consecutive order) found in the paragraph above should be written on this line. _____

These letters spell out a famous place along the Hudson River in New York _____,

something your body needs _____, and a famous trio, namely

_____.

15. THE TWENTY-FIVE PREPOSITIONAL PHRASES

How many of the twenty-five prepositional phrases found in these fifteen sentences can you find? Underline these twenty-five prepositional phrases. Not every sentence contains a prepositional phrase.

1. In the morning mom drives Maureen to school.

2. Without our approval, the television program was videotaped on Tuesday night at ten o'clock.

3. Over the river and through the woods to grandmother's house we go.

4. He wanted to go, but his mother said he couldn't.

5. To be or not to be.

6. Everybody who is sitting near the door must now move beyond the tables.

7. None of the bread that we bought in the city is here on the counter.

8. Look under the couch and by the bureau.

9. Lance threw the ball to the first baseman wearing the striped shirt.

10. The children in the elementary school orchestra waited without their director for a quarter of an hour.

11. Sit between Tricia and me.

12. Before you leave the house, walk past your room and look at the cat.

13. Run there and tell us what is happening.

14. It is certainly not surprising that you and I were picked to be lab partners.

15. This was bought by your uncle for two hundred dollars.

16. FANBOY AND W.N. BEN

These combinations of letters in the activity's title function as a mnemonic, a way to remember conjunctions. They are the first letters of eleven conjunctions. For, And, Nor, But, Or, and Yet are conjunctions. The team conjunctions are Whether...or, Neither...nor, Both...and, Either....or, and Not only....but also. Conjunctions, as you know, join words or groups of words.

Circle the conjunctions in these sentences and be ready to explain what the conjunctions join.

1. Would you please buy me a poster and the group's new CD?

2. Either the team members or the manager will sign autographs for the fans.

3. Mr. Parker would usually be there, but he has to attend a wedding this weekend.

4. We can see the movie in Pottsfield or New Lake.

5. Birds migrate south for they seek a warmer climate in the winter.

6. He not only wrote the book, but he also published it himself.

7. We enjoyed both the novel and the movie version of *The Outsiders*.

8. Neither the First Amendment question nor the Fifth Amendment question was an easy one.

9. Monica wanted to go to Florida during the winter recess, but her parents were against the plan.

10. The podiatrist asked whether I preferred swimming or biking.

11. I don't want to watch the television show, nor do I want you to tell me what it was about.

17. SUBORDINATING CONJUNCTIONS

Subordinating conjunctions introduce adverb clauses. In the sentence, "We went to the movies after we had soccer practice," the word **after** is the subordinating conjunction that introduces the adverb clause **after we had soccer practice**. An adverb clause is a subordinate clause that modifies a verb, adjective, or adverb. The letters of the twenty subordinating conjunctions have been scrambled. Unscramble them and write each subordinating conjunction correctly in the spaces provided.

1. EWHHERT   1. _ _ _ _ _ _ _
2. REAFT   2. _ _ _ _ _
3. EBUSCEA   3. _ _ _ _ _ _ _
4. ECINS   4. _ _ _ _ _
5. UHGATLHO   5. _ _ _ _ _ _ _ _
6. UHHGTO   6. _ _ _ _ _ _
7. EERWVEHN   7. _ _ _ _ _ _ _ _
8. HEREW   8. _ _ _ _ _
9. SA   9. _ _
10. ETHVAREW   10. _ _ _ _ _ _ _ _
11. OEBREF   11. _ _ _ _ _ _
12. EWNH   12. _ _ _ _
13. SLESNU   13. _ _ _ _ _ _
14. HTNA   14. _ _ _ _
15. FI   15. _ _
16. SLTE   16. _ _ _ _
17. HATT   17. _ _ _ _
18. TLUNI   18. _ _ _ _ _
19. EVEEWRRH   19. _ _ _ _ _ _ _ _
20. LWIHE   20. _ _ _ _ _

18. SIMPLE SUBJECTS AND THE HIDDEN SENTENCE

Underline the simple subject in each sentence. Then write in consecutive order the first two letters of each sentence's simple subject on the line below the last question. If you have done it correctly, you will have a seven-word sentence. What is the sentence? Good luck!

1. Certain thermometers in this carton need to be placed on the shelves.

2. Has the most important issue been discussed yet?

3. The mouse's timidity in this case does not surprise me.

4. Measurements during the football game drag the game out considerably.

5. Wesley refuses to tolerate such immature behavior.

6. In the wet and snowy winter months, this carpet takes a beating.

7. Natives will come and greet you.

8. With the right kind of camera, the sky can be photographed beautifully.

9. They can hardly complete the project without our help.

10. John's embarrassment could easily be detected by those around him.

11. Anyone in this car can keep a mileage chart.

Write the first two letters of each subject, in consecutive order, here. _____

What does the sentence say? _____

19. CONSTRUCTING SENTENCES

Here is your chance to construct ten sentences, but there is a catch! You must follow some directions. Each blank has a part of speech underneath it. Fill in the blank with a word that is that part of speech. The sentences must have all the blanks filled in and must make sense. If you successfully construct seven, eight, or nine sentences, you have had a good day. Ten sentences done perfectly means you have had an outstanding day!

1. _____ _____ _____ _____ _____ .
   pronoun   verb   preposition   adjective   noun

2. _____ _____ _____ _____ _____ .
   noun   helping verb   verb   adjective   noun

3. _____ _____ _____ _____ _____ .
   noun   conjunction   pronoun   verb   adverb

4. _____ _____ _____ _____ ?
  helping verb   pronoun   verb   pronoun

5. _____ _____ _____ _____ _____ _____ .
   pronoun   conjunction   noun   helping verb   verb   pronoun

6. _____ _____ _____ _____ _____ .
   pronoun   adverb   verb   adjective   noun

7. _____ _____ _____ _____ .
   adverb   verb   adjective   noun

8. _____ _____ _____ _____ _____ _____ ?
  helping verb   pronoun   verb   pronoun   preposition   noun

9. _____ _____ _____ _____ _____ _____ _____ .
   adjective   noun helping verb   verb   adjective   noun   adverb

10. _____ _____ _____ _____ .
   verb   pronoun   preposition   noun

© 1998 by John Wiley & Sons, Inc

20. FILL AND COMPLETE

Each of these sentences will be complete once you have supplied a missing word. Although each word can be one of your choice, the word's part of speech can only be one of the eight parts of speech. Fill in the blanks with a word and then write the word's part of speech in the blank after the question's number. A part of speech may be used more than once. The first one is done for you. The eight parts of speech are listed below.

adjective (adj)   conjunction (c)   noun (n)   pronoun (p)

adverb (advb)   interjection (i)   preposition (prep)   verb (v)

1. __noun__   The swift <u>runner</u> finished the race in just over two hours and twenty minutes.

2. _____   She had _____ for two years for this important race.

3. _____   The runner felt that _____ had done her best to be in top shape for this event.

4. _____   Feeling _____ confident, she started the race in the lead pack of runners.

5. _____   The _____ runners in the world were running up in the front with her.

6. _____   As she was running _____ this group, she tried to read what each runner in the pack was thinking.

7. _____   She wanted to push herself harder, _____ she knew she had to conserve her energy for the last few miles.

8. _____   When she neared the twenty-five mile marker, she _____ more confident that she might win the race.

9. _____   Knowing the others were tired, she gave it her best effort to _____ them out.

10. _____   The following day's newspaper headline read, "_____! Marathon Champion Sets New Course Record"

21. SAME WORD...DIFFERENT PART OF SPEECH

Identify the part of speech for each of the underlined words, then write its part of speech in the space before each sentence. If you have correctly identified each underlined word's part of speech, you will find four nouns, three prepositions, three verbs, two adjectives, two adverbs, and one conjunction.

1. _____ The meteorologist predicted heavy <u>snow</u> for this winter.

2. _____ I could not find the <u>snow</u> shovel in the garage.

3. _____ Do you think it will <u>snow</u> this much this winter?

4. _____ I wore my jacket made of <u>down</u> during the cold winter last year.

5. _____ We saw Manny <u>down</u> a warm drink after he shoveled.

6. _____ Katrina fell <u>down</u> the stairs while she was rushing to get her boots.

7. _____ After seeing that much snow on the ground, Yves wanted to get <u>down</u> to work.

8. _____ Our family made the <u>down</u> payment on the snow plow.

9. _____ Ursula walked <u>out</u> the door to help her sister clear a path to the cars.

10. _____ She had to search <u>around</u> for her gloves.

11. _____ The neighborhood children ran <u>around</u> the corner chasing each other.

12. _____ <u>While</u> they were outside, the children had a great time in the snow.

13. _____ They didn't come indoors for a long <u>while</u>.

14. _____ Olivia's <u>smile</u> told her mom that she was happy playing outdoors.

15. _____ Her mother could only <u>smile</u> when she saw her kids so happy outdoors.

22. DOUBLE-DUTY WORDS

Seventeen five-letter words, each beginning with a different letter of the alphabet, can be found in this puzzle. Each word can be used as at least two different parts of speech. The words are placed backwards, forward, diagonally, and up and down. The first letters of the included words are listed below. Circle each word and then write it in the appropriate space below the puzzle.

```
K X D V M Y Z Z Z B Y B W Q S Q H S Q T P M C V
F M M X F F M N R M S B P C F K V Y W T Z C N G
R H D X J V M G V Y G B X P Q D L S S S Q S Y K
Z L W N G Y B Z V P N Y Q L F T M R R Q O H N Z
E M P N W V R J L O Q C K U F R L E Y G R F X W
N L Z W T X E X V W N Y P N O Q O F R G B T A K
R U E D M D A F F E C N N S S T W D X I I S M C
P V D C F S K H U R R Y K N I F E T R T T P M K
G A L G T F J B A S K S B V R M R C U E S T Q J
P L J V E S S W D Q T Q D O A E D P N A A G D L
H U B C W C L R X B L D W H A T N S R A G D H Y
S E Z D D J N R Y N V N S T W I V G R T L K R D
V R F J N R F W H J P Z B T M J C M X W W N L P
B G D F S T J T M W B H F R T W D Y H L R S Q M
M Z P H P N S B M P B K X J C G M C P B J Z F W
L N V Y N B T P B Q V S Z H Q K Q Y X G G N C N
D H C F C G X H D K H S G N P Q D W W B P C L B
```

B _____   H _____   N _____   V _____

C _____   I _____   O _____   W _____

D _____   K _____   P _____

E _____   L _____   Q _____

G _____   M _____   S _____

23. WIN, PLACE, AND SHOW

The race is on! These ten words are vying for first, second, and third places. Write the number "3" before any word that can be at least three parts of speech, the number "2" next to a word that is only two parts of speech (no more and no less than two), and the number "1" next to a word that can be only one part of speech. Those words that score a three win; those that score two place; those that earn one point show. Write the word's part(s) of speech in the space after the word.

1. _____ bid _____

2. _____ down _____

3. _____ into _____

4. _____ key _____

5. _____ major _____

6. _____ pick _____

7. _____ retail _____

8. _____ severe _____

9. _____ snow _____

10. _____ token _____

A six-way tie for first place includes the words _____, _____, _____, _____, _____, and _____.

Second-place winners are _____ and _____.

Those that placed third are _____ and _____.

24. PARTS OF SPEECH MAGIC SQUARE

Test your knowledge of the eight parts of speech by matching the description with its appropriate word. Thus, the description number that matches up with the word **tree** (letter A's word) will be placed in the appropriate box within the Magic Square. When your answers are correct, all columns and rows will add to the same number.

A. TREE   E. CLEVERLY   I. HAMPERED   M. MOOSE

B. WAS   F. PRETTY   J. HERD   N. HENRY

C. DOWN   G. SHE   K. GOSH   O. INTO

D. ANYONE   H. NOR   L. HIMSELF   P. ABOUT

1. adjective
2. past tense verb
3. preposition
4. indefinite pronoun
5. noun whose singular and plural are spelled the same
6. helping verb
7. conjunction
8. interjection

9. can be used as five parts of speech
10. preposition and adverb
11. collective noun
12. adverb
13. reflexive pronoun
14. third person singular pronoun
15. common noun
16. proper noun

A	B	C	D
E	F	G	H
I	J	K	L
M	N	O	P

25. GRAMMAR REVIEW

How well do you know your adjectives, prepositions, verbs, and subjects? Identify each of these in the sentences below by drawing a box around the prepositions, an X over the adjectives, a circle around the subjects, and underlining the main verbs.

1. He knew the correct answer to the difficult problem.

2. The magician cleverly performed the trick during the show.

3. Throughout my childhood, I played the guitar and the piano.

4. This is not a story about a new movie.

5. We wheeled the patient past the crowded room.

6. My mother had smelled smoke in the kitchen.

7. It is written with his trademark style.

8. The play is a comedy written by a famous playwright.

9. All of the money was found near the desk.

10. I definitely received very little information from him.

26. WILL THE REAL GERALD R. FORD PLEASE STAND UP?

Is President Gerald R. Ford really Gerald R. Ford? If you know your parts of speech and the nominative, objective and possessive cases, you will soon find out. Your answers will be based on the sentence directly below this paragraph. Circle the letter next to each correct answer and then write the letter after the last question. The letters will spell out the answer to the question, "What was President Gerald R. Ford's birth name?"

When Sly had finished his art project, he went to his friend's house to help her pack for camp.

1. Which word is a proper noun?   (J) camp   (K) over   (L) Sly

2. A helping verb is   (D) pack   (E) had   (F) went.

3. Which word is the subject of the dependent clause?   (S) Sly   (T) he   (U) house

4. The infinitive is   (L) to help   (M) to his   (N) for camp.

5. Which word is a possessive pronoun?   (H) he   (I) his   (J) for

6. In this sentence *pack* is used as a   (C) noun   (D) adverb   (E) verb.

7. Which word is NOT used in the nominative case?   (J) Sly   (K) he   (L) friend's

8. Which word is NOT used in the possessive case?   (X) his   (Y) he   (Z) friend's

9. What is the main verb in the dependent clause?   (N) finished   (O) went   (P) help

10. A prepositional phrase is   (C) for camp   (D) his art project   (E) went to his.

11. A word used in the objective case is   (F) finished   (G) pack   (H) project.

12. A subordinating conjunction is   (J) went   (K) When   (L) art.

13. The subject of the independent clause is   (I) he   (J) Sly   (K) her.

14. The tense of the word *went* is   (L) present   (M) future   (N) past.

15. If the comma were replaced by a period, there now would be   (G) a fragment followed by a complete sentence   (H) a comma splice   (I) two fragments.

16. A word that is both a pronoun and an adjective in this sentence is   (I) art   (J) his   (K) her.

17. Two prepositions in this sentence are   (P) had and to   (Q) went and for   (R) to and for.

What was President Gerald R. Ford's birth name?

_____

27. GRAMMAR AND USAGE CROSSWORD

Questions dealing with grammar and usage are found below. For certain questions, refer to the word(s) underlined within the sentence. Fill in your answers.

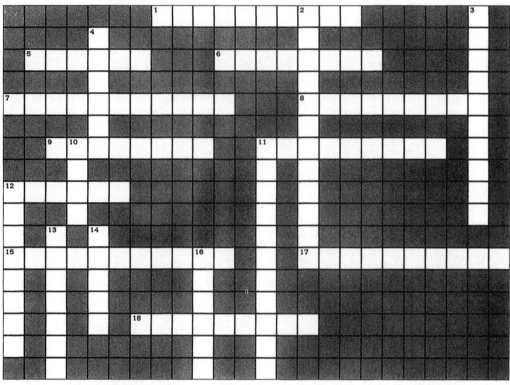

ACROSS

1. Lance wanted <u>to win first prize</u>.
   (_____ phrase)

5. Queen Mary wore the <u>crown</u>.
   (_____ object)

6. Who, whom, whose and that are called
   _____ pronouns.

7. <u>Or</u> is always what part of speech?

8. Himself, yourself and ourselves are called
   _____ pronouns.

9. You could have given <u>him</u> the CD.
   (_____ object)

11. Tom is my <u>coach</u>. (_____ noun)

12. The older teacher <u>who helped us out</u> is new
    to the school. (adjective _____)

15. <u>Walking down the corridor</u>, Kyle was
    laughing. (_____ phrase)

17. <u>They</u> is always used in the _____
    case.

18. Yvonne was <u>happy</u>. (predicate _____)

DOWN

2. Ugh! I think I broke my thumb.
   (Ugh! is an _____)

3. Their, my and his are pronouns used
   in the _____ case.

4. <u>Walking into a crowded room</u> is not
   easy for Geraldo.
   (_____ phrase)

10. Len remembers <u>what he said</u>,
    (_____ clause)

11. Adriana brought the car to the <u>mall</u>.
    (object of the _____)

12. <u>You</u> and <u>she</u> make a cute couple.
    (_____ subject)

13. <u>You</u> is always what part of speech?

14. <u>I</u> is a _____ person
    pronoun.

16. <u>Whenever he is sleepy</u>, he gets silly.
    (_____ clause)

28. FINAL TEST ON CONJUNCTIONS AND PREPOSITIONS

PART ONE: CONJUNCTIONS

Directions: Find ten conjunctions within these sentences. They may be coordinating, correlative or subordinating conjunctions. The two parts of the correlative conjunctions (either...or) will count as one. Underline each conjunction. Then at the bottom of the page, write the conjunction in the appropriate space corresponding to the sentence number. Each conjunction is worth five points.

1. The couple will not move until their new house is completely finished.
2. Both the husband and the wife decided that they wanted to live in North Carolina.
3. Before they married, they met in college and spent much time together.
4. Not only did they want to live by the water, but they also wanted to live near a college.
5. When the chance to move to a new house came along, they didn't hesitate for they knew it was the best move for them.
6. As they were saving for their house, they worked extra hours and saved most of their overtime pay.
7. Because the couple worked so hard, their dreams came true.

PART TWO: PREPOSITIONS

Directions: Underline the ten prepositional phrases in these sentences. At the bottom of the page, write each phrase in the appropriate space corresponding to the sentence number. Each sentence contains at least one prepositional phrase. Each phrase is worth five points.

1. Hal likes skiing on Mount Draper in the morning.
2. After the last time he went skiing, Hal fell asleep early that night.
3. Snow fell throughout the day.
4. His sister Fran and her friends went to Florida during the recent winter recess.
5. She swam before breakfast each day and stayed indoors until the hot part of the day was over.
6. The temperature was above ninety degrees each day.
7. Many people on the beach played volleyball.

Conjunctions (10 at 5 points each)

1. _____
2. _____
3. _____
4. _____
5. _____
6. _____
7. _____

Prepositional Phrases (10 at 5 points each)

1. _____
2. _____
3. _____
4. _____
5. _____
6. _____
7. _____

Conjunction Score _____

Prepositional Phrase Score _____

Final Score (Conjunction and Prepositional Phrase Scores) _____

29. FINAL TEST ON PARTS OF SPEECH

Identify the part of speech of each underlined word below. Write your answer in the space before the sentence. The eight parts of speech are listed below. Each correct answer is worth five points. Good luck!

adjective	conjunction	noun	pronoun
adverb	interjection	preposition	verb

1. _____ The <u>concert</u> was held in the large arena.

2. _____ Many people <u>were</u> in attendance that night.

3. _____ Ads for the concert had been placed in the newspapers for weeks <u>before</u> the event.

4. _____ Tickets were quickly bought and the concert was sold out almost <u>immediately</u>.

5. _____ Thousands of <u>excited</u> people lined up at least five hours before the doors were opened.

6. _____ My friends and <u>I</u> waited anxiously for the concert to start.

7. _____ Neither the security guards <u>nor</u> the concert organizers expected any trouble.

8. _____ <u>During</u> the three-hour concert the group did many of their standard songs.

9. _____ The concession stands were crowded since many of <u>us</u> were hungry and thirsty.

10. _____ Grabbing the microphone, the lead singer told the crowd to clap their <u>hands</u> loudly.

11. _____ "<u>Awesome</u>!" shouted the bass guitar player as the clapping became louder and louder.

12. _____ The <u>tallest</u> people in the crowd made it hard for some of us to see the stage.

13. _____ <u>Nobody</u> misbehaved at all.

14. _____ Unfortunately one of the amplifiers blew a fuse <u>about</u> an hour into the performance.

15. _____ <u>Each</u> of the six band members worked enthusiastically to make the crowd happy.

16. _____ I could not <u>wait</u> to hear them do my favorite song.

17. _____ Surely everyone was hoping that the night would <u>not</u> end.

18. _____ Immediately before their last song the group thanked the audience members for their behavior and <u>enthusiasm</u>.

19. _____ All of the people were <u>ecstatic</u> when the band finished the last number.

20. _____ We will never forget how much fun we <u>had</u> that night.

© 1998 by John Wiley & Sons, Inc

30. FINAL TEST ON PHRASES AND CLAUSES

Directions: Each of these twenty sentences contains an italicized phrase or clause. In the appropriate space next to each number, write the letter that corresponds to the correct phrase or clause from the list below. A letter may be used more than once. Each correct answer is worth five points.

A. independent clause
B. adjective clause
C. adverb clause
D. noun clause

E. verb phrase
F. adjective phrase
G. adverb phrase
H. participial phrase

I. infinitive phrase
J. gerund phrase

1. _____ *What he did* was correct.

2. _____ He will often go for a jog *in the afternoon*.

3. _____ The woman, *whom I introduced to you*, is the store manager.

4. _____ After he won the election, *Rudy thanked his election campaign committee*.

5. _____ This is the car *which he bought with his own money*.

6. _____ Whenever I begin to feel nervous, *I think of something I like to do*.

7. _____ None of us wanted *to leave the car*.

8. _____ *Finding the criminal* was the officer's goal.

9. _____ He *had completed* the project in several hours.

10. _____ Warren felt *that he would be the captain of the lacrosse team*.

11. _____ The deer were running *toward the stream*.

12. _____ *My mother and father will go to the casino* if the bus is not crowded.

13. _____ The car *with the clever license plate* is hers.

14. _____ *Walking toward the corner*, Manny saw his friends near the store.

15. _____ *Nearing the end of the marathon* made Roberto happy.

16. _____ The cat *near the desk* is the one I found in the park.

17. _____ The giraffe, *scared by the lights of the cameras*, began to panic.

18. _____ *To nominate only the best candidate* was Jim's goal.

19. _____ The number of clerks in the store had increased *since the holiday season shopping was heavy*.

20. _____ *After the musicians packed up their equipment*, they began their trip to the next concert's location.

Final Score : Number correct _____ x 5 = _____

Section Two

USAGE

31. DID I DO GOOD OR DID I DO WELL?

You might have debated which one of these questions is correct. "Did I do well?" is the better question since well is the adverb that answers the question, "How did you do?"

Here are fifteen sentences that contain words that are often confused. These words have been placed on two teams. Circle the correct word in each sentence, see which team it is on, and credit that team with the number of points in parentheses found next to the sentences. Then tally up the number of points earned by each team. Declare the winner in the designated space here. And the winner is Team _____.

Team A: affect, beside, between, bring, discover, fewer, good, learn, leave, like, than

Team B: among, as, besides, effect, invent, less, let, take, teach, then, well

A. (1)   How will this (affect, effect) my final grade?

B. (2)   (Beside, Besides) Moe, how many others are going to the concert?

C. (2)   Please divide the cookies (among, between) the five of us.

D. (1)   (Bring, Take) the book back here as soon as possible.

E. (1)   Did Curie (discover, invent) radium?

F. (1)   This year's season has three (fewer, less) days than last season.

G. (2)   The students did as (good, well) as they did on the exam last year.

H. (2)   Can you (learn, teach) us that material dealing with a country's economics?

I. (1)   (Leave, Let) us alone!

J. (1)   He says there is nobody (as, like) his mother.

K. (1)   Richard is two inches taller (than, then) his brother.

L. (2)   What is the principal (affect, effect) of the war?

M. (2)   (Bring, Take) this package to the post office.

N. (2)   I did the project (as, like) I was told to do it.

O. (1)   The goods were divided (among, between) the four hunters.

32. DID THE DOE EAT THE DOUGH?

Words that sound the same but are spelled differently are the order of the day in this activity. Match each of these sixteen words with its correct definition. Write your answers in the Magic Square below. If all your answers are correct, all columns and rows will total the same number. When finished with the Magic Square, write each word's homophone on the reverse side of the paper.

A. BIER   E. INTENTS   I. LEASED   M. GROAN
B. STAIR   F. FLOWER   J. WASTE   N. BRED
C. ARK   G. WREST   K. HIRE   O. DOUGH
D. AURAL   H. MINOR   L. CYMBAL   P. CHEWS

1. bread mixture   9. juvenile
2. by ear   10. employ
3. garbage   11. coffin
4. aims   12. cultivated
5. rented   13. step
6. plant   14. moan
7. bites   15. take from
8. boat   16. instrument

A	B	C	D
E	F	G	H
I	J	K	L
M	N	O	P

33. WHOM DO YOU TRUST?

Whether to use *who* or *whom* poses a problem for some. This activity will help to clarify the situation. Match the words in Column A with the best blank in the sentences in Column B. Each word in Column A is used only once. The first one is done for you.

COLUMN A		COLUMN B
1. __D__ BESIDES	A.	_____ packages were sent out this week.
2. _____ BESIDE	B.	What did you _____ from what the speaker was saying?
3. _____ WHO	C.	Our coach took a(n) _____ approach to the problem.
4. _____ LESS	D.	Only a few came to help, and _____, we can try to get new workers tomorrow.
5. _____ COMPLEMENT	E.	Most of the people at the park were _____ in what the rude people were doing.
6. _____ FEWER	F.	Rarely will that teacher not _____ a student for a good deed.
7. _____ AMONG	G.	_____ enthusiasm was shown at the rally.
8. _____ UNINTERESTED	H.	Louie and Tricia sat _____ one another.
9. _____ IMPLY	I.	The _____ of the matter is what bothers her the most.
10. _____ INFER	J.	One of the men _____ said that will be here soon.
11. _____ PRINCIPLE	K.	The extra hundred dollars was divided _____ the seven people who helped out.
12. _____ COMPLIMENT	L.	Who will be the _____ speaker at this year's convention?
13. _____ BETWEEN	M.	Their musical and singing abilities _____ one another.
14. _____ DISINTERESTED	N.	The candy was divided _____ the two children.
15. _____ WHOM	O.	Did the speaker _____ that he was going to resign?
16. _____ PRINCIPAL	P.	The man to _____ I was speaking is your new boss.

© 1998 by John Wiley & Sons, Inc

34. A MAGIC SQUARE FEATURING WORDS THAT ARE OFTEN CONFUSED

What is the difference between **principal** and **principle**? When does one **infer** and when does one **imply**? If you know the answers to these questions, you are off to a good start to solving the Magic Square. Complete each sentence with the correct word from the Word Bank. Write your word's letter answer in the appropriate space within the square. If your answers are correct, all columns and rows will add up to the same number.

A	B	C	D
E	F	G	H
I	J	K	L
M	N	O	P

A. WHOSE	E. ADVISE	I. WHO'S	M. LED
B. QUITE	F. THAN	J. IMPLY	N. LEAD
C. IT'S	G. ITS	K. PRINCIPLE	O. QUIET
D. PRINCIPAL	H. INFER	L. ADVICE	P. THEN

1. Did you _____ from the speaker's words that she was displeased?
2. We were _____ in the wrong direction by them.
3. The runners were _____ tired after completing the marathon.
4. The _____ of gravity is interesting.
5. What did the speaker _____ by her words?
6. _____ starting to rain.
7. She was _____ an amateur softball player.
8. I think I will need to _____ you on how to cast your fishing line.
9. Please be _____ in the library.
10. Hector is younger _____ Michelle.
11. Do they know _____ knocking on the door?
12. Who is the building's _____?
13. _____ jacket was missing?
14. Did you heed your sister's _____?
15. The dog hurt _____ tail.
16. _____ is a metal.

35. DOES THIS STORY HAVE A MORALE?

This activity's title should have been proofread because the word **morale** should really be **moral**. These twenty sentences deal with words that are often confused. Underline the correct word in each sentence. If you have answered all questions correctly, you will have selected the first word of the two available choices eight times.

1. Ursula has to (adapt, adopt) quickly to her new surroundings.

2. Will her mother's job (affect, effect) her staying after school for clubs?

3. Both of Ursula's sisters attended the (bazaar, bizarre) at the school last Saturday.

4. They (preceded, proceeded) to go from one booth to another.

5. At the movies Ursula saw the manager who tried to calm the (indigenous, indignant) patron who was yelling about something.

6. Ursula was (incredible, incredulous) at what she saw that night at the movies.

7. The manager tried to calm the angered customer (least, lest) something ugly happen.

8. One of the assistant managers attempted to (quiet, quite) the crowd.

9. None of the people watching the scene became (fiscal, physical).

10. (All together, Altogether) the scene lasted about four minutes.

11. Two of the workers (detracted, distracted) the people watching the argument.

12. The crowd quickly and gently (disbursed, dispersed) from the lobby.

13. On Sunday afternoon Ursula's mother read about a local (cooperation, corporation) that was raising funds for a community park.

14. She wanted to (command, commend) the owners for their community concern.

15. The (area, aria) could certainly use the help of that maintenance crew.

16. How much better the (annual, annul) fair would be if it were held in a beautifully landscaped park!

17. What a (deference, difference) this would make in the town!

18. The citizens would now take more pride in (their, there) community.

19. To what (extant, extent) this park would raise property values was not yet known.

20. Obviously, a new community spirit was (emerging, immerging)!

36. WRITE THE RIGHT WORDS

Each sentence has two blanks. These blanks should be filled in with words that are homophones. Write the correct words in the blanks. The first one is done for you.

1. The __seller__ stored her merchandise in the __cellar__.

2. I couldn't _____ to look at the _____ that had mauled the zookeeper.

3. We heard the _____ about how the dog caught his _____ in the door.

4. _____ of us felt that the _____ was not a holy person.

5. _____ goal is to jog for an _____.

6. The _____ _____ all the beds on our hotel floor by noon.

7. I somehow _____ that the _____ dog would need to be trained.

8. The boss promised us construction workers a _____ if we could _____ the tall building in a day.

9. Ivan had to _____ down after _____ splattered on his face.

10. The store held a _____ on the _____ I want to buy for my boat.

11. The doctor said my _____ will _____ in a week if I don't put too much pressure on it.

12. Seeing the empty table, the restaurant manager _____ that the _____ had left without paying his bill.

13. Monty does _____ know how to tie a _____.

14. Did you _____ what the senator said _____ today?

15. Does it _____ that the _____ of her dress is crooked?

37. IRREGULAR VERBS

When you were a child just learning the English language, you might have thought that the past tense of the verb **swim** was **swimmed**. Swim is one of those verbs called "irregular" since it doesn't form its past or past participle in the usual fashion by adding the **-ed** ending to the present tense. The past tense of the verb **swim** is **swam** and its past participle is **swum**.

This activity features the past participles of twenty irregular verbs. The letters of the past participles of twenty irregular verbs are found in Column A. Unscramble the letters and then write the present tense verb in Column B.

Column A	Column B
1. ESCNHO	1. _____
2. NURKD	2. _____
3. NUEBG	3. _____
4. UBTRHGO	4. _____
5. HOWNRT	5. _____
6. RVEID	6. _____
7. NSGU	7. _____
8. EBTTNI	8. _____
9. OECM	9. _____
10. ENETA	10. _____
11. NOWFL	11. _____
12. VGENI	12. _____
13. ENTWITR	13. _____
14. NGUR	14. _____
15. UMWS	15. _____
16. WANDR	16. _____
17. ASDI	17. _____
18. NLTEOS	18. _____
19. ONED	19. _____
20. ELNFAL	20. _____

38. MORE IRREGULAR VERBS

Twenty irregular verbs are found in this cryptolist. Find the letters that were substituted in the original word and write the irregular verb in the appropriate spaces. As you work on trying to identify the irregular verbs, use the Letter Substitution Code found below the last question.

1.	ZHEOH	=	_ _ _ _ _
2.	JEVK	=	_ _ _ _
3.	CEKKWH	=	_ _ _ _ _ _
4.	JWL	=	_ _ _
5.	JWHK	=	_ _ _ _
6.	VTMZWH	=	_ _ _ _ _ _
7.	UQEZWH	=	_ _ _ _ _ _
8.	CEHW	=	_ _ _ _
9.	CQEOH	=	_ _ _ _ _
10.	VWWH	=	_ _ _ _
11.	QSLLWH	=	_ _ _ _ _ _
12.	RJIHC	=	_ _ _ _ _
13.	UWMKWH	=	_ _ _ _ _ _
14.	NMICTK	=	_ _ _ _ _ _
15.	RQEGWH	=	_ _ _ _ _ _
16.	VKIHC	=	_ _ _ _ _
17.	NQWBK	=	_ _ _ _ _
18.	QIH	=	_ _ _
19.	UIQVK	=	_ _ _ _ _
20.	UEQHW	=	_ _ _ _ _

Letter Substitution Code Used:

Letter: A B C D E F G H I J K L M N O P Q R S T U V W X Y Z

Code: _ _ _ _ R _ _ _ _ _ _ _ _ _ E _ _ _ _ _ I _ _ _ _ _

39. IRREGULAR VERBS AND THREE COUNTRIES

These eighteen questions deal with irregular verbs. The infinitive form of the irregular verb is in parentheses after the question's number. Write the correct form of the word in the blanks within each sentence. Then unscramble the eighteen circled letters to form the names of three countries that begin with the same letter.

1. (deal)   He was _ _ ◯ _ _ a bad hand of cards.
2. (spin)   Lonnie _ _ ◯ _ the wheel.
3. (sting)   Nobody was _ _ _ _ ◯ by the wasps found in our backyard.
4. (spring)   The animal _ _ ◯ _ _ _ up at us when we searched the woods.
5. (spit)   Jerry _ ◯ _ _ out the dirt that he had in his mouth after the tackle.
6. (ring)   Has the bell _ ◯ _ _ yet?
7. (weep)   All of us _ ◯ _ _ when we heard the sad news.
8. (swim)   I never _ _ ◯ _ in Bailey's Lake before today.
9. (draw)   Are all the caricatures _ _ _ _ ◯ well?
10. (catch)   Two criminals have already been _ ◯ _ _ _ _.
11. (drink)   Both of the runners _ _ ◯ _ _ from the same cup during the marathon.
12. (slide)   Have you ever _ ◯ _ _ and fallen down in front of a crowd?
13. (speak)   I thought he _ ◯ _ _ _ to you about the new bike.
14. (swim)   The champion swimmer has never _ _ _ ◯ that far before today.
15. (wear)   Haven't you already _ _ ◯ _ that outfit this week?
16. (tear)   Unfortunately, this uniform has been _ ◯ _ _ in two places.
17. (sleep)   My grandfather _ _ _ ◯ _ in my brother's room last night.
18. (get)   You know you could easily have _ _ _ ◯ _ _ hurt by doing what you did.

The eighteen circled letters are:

_ _ _ _ _ _ _ _ _ _ _ _ _ _ _ _ _ _

The three countries these letters form are: _____, _____, and
_____ .

40. HOW MANY N'S ARE THERE?

Thirteen irregular verbs are scrambled in the following sentences. In the space after each sentence, write the correct spelling of the scrambled word. Then circle the last letter of the word and write it on the line below question 13. If you have the correct answers, the letter that appears most often on the line is *n*. How many times does it appear? Write your answer below.

1. Last night we <u>vrdoe</u> to Eddie's house. _____

2. We had <u>nsgu</u> that song more than twenty times. _____

3. Most of us <u>etwp</u> after hearing about her death. _____

4. The fabric has certainly been intricately <u>nowev</u>. _____

5. The group had been <u>keshan</u> by the earth's rumblings. _____

6. One of the prisoners was <u>dehnag</u> at noon in the town square. _____

7. A heavy package had been <u>obnre</u> by the mule. _____

8. Our team has been <u>nebtae</u> by your team in the championship game. _____

9. Roger's coat had been <u>heiddn</u> in the hall closet. _____

10. We had <u>npsu</u> the wheel before so it wasn't a problem. _____

11. The board had been <u>esptw</u> away by the strong tides. _____

12. During the very cold winter the pipe had <u>usbtr</u>. _____

13. Joan's cat had <u>laeepd</u> upon my lap during the meal. _____

The circled letters are: _____

The letter *n* appears _____ times.

41. ACTIVE AND PASSIVE VOICES

The active voice has challenged the passive voice to a contest. The winner will be the voice that has the most points. The voice that is used in the question is awarded the point value found in parentheses before the question number. Use the tally space below the last question and declare a winner. Will it be the active voice or the passive voice?

(2)   1. The students were carefully chosen.

(3)   2. Our coach diagrammed a play for us to use.

(2)   3. Wendy was selected as the group's representative.

(1)   4. *The Adventures of Tom Sawyer* was written by Mark Twain.

(2)   5. I ignored the silly rules.

(3)   6. The entire first act was written by Kate and Jamey.

(2)   7. One of the guests left his scarf in the den.

(3)   8. Each of the musicians was given a medal after the performance.

(1)   9. He was not recognized by anybody yesterday.

(2) 10. The teacher's briefcase has been missing since Tuesday.

(1) 11. I will always remember your clever jokes.

(1) 12. The gymnast carefully planned her routine for the state competition.

(3) 13. Senators from many states voted against the changes.

(3) 14. A brilliant flash of light temporarily blinded us.

(2) 15. The news of the victory was received with delight.

Points won by the Active Voice: _____

Points won by the Passive Voice: _____

And the winner is the _____ Voice!

42. POSITIVE...COMPARATIVE...SUPERLATIVE

Modifiers change as they are used in comparison. The three degrees of comparison are: **positive**, **comparative**, and **superlative**. If the positive form of the word *large* is *large*, the comparative form is *larger*, and its superlative form is *largest*. Some modifiers will use the word *more* for the comparative and *most* for the superlative.

In this activity, you are given the positive form of comparison in parentheses. In the space within each sentence, fill in the correct form of the modifier.

1. (happy)   She is _____ now than she has ever been.

2. (recent)   This is the _____ version of the story.

3. (beautiful)   She is the _____ girl I have ever met!

4. (young)   Who is the _____ man to be elected to that position?

5. (useful)   The tape measure is one of the _____ tools a carpenter uses.

6. (simple)   Of all the methods I know, this is definitely the _____.

7. (bad)   Though he earned a bad grade on yesterday's test, his grade today is even _____.

8. (practical)   Of all the great designers, Kevin is one of the _____ designers to come along.

9. (often)   Tracy tends to attend the meetings _____ now.

10. (good)   There is a _____ way to solve the math problem.

11. (favorably)   We reacted _____ to the news than they had.

12. (pretty)   This vacation spot is _____ than the Blasely Mountain retreat.

13. (soon)   We will probably arrive _____ than you.

14. (many)   There are _____ pigeons here today.

15. (rough)   His brother is _____ than Luke is.

43. MODIFYING THE MODIFIERS

Each of the twelve sentences below has a modifier that is used incorrectly. On the space below each sentence, write the corrected form of the sentence. The first one is done for you.

1. In the bottom of the bottle, I noticed that the drink had dried up.

   <u>I noticed that the drink had dried up in the bottom of the bottle.</u>

2. While cleaning the bathroom, the phone rang.

   _____

3. The boys saw the magician performing his tricks in our van.

   _____

4. Inside the freezer, Marcia detected an unpleasant smell.

   _____

5. We watched him score the basket from the window.

   _____

6. From inside the car's engine, I heard the noise.

   _____

7. Eating our cat's food, Dad spotted the neighbor's cat.

   _____

8. We sell shoes to senior high school students with rubber soles.

   _____

9. The scientist saw the moon looking through her telescope.

   _____

10. The bulb was fixed by the man in the flashlight.

    _____

11. The hostess served the steak to the guests on her finest plates.

    _____

12. Walking to school, the bus was spotted by the children.

    _____

44. DOUBLE NEGATIVES

Once upon a time, in one of their hit songs, The Rolling Stones rock group sang, "I can't get no satisfaction." This is an example of a double negative problem since **can't** and **no** are both negative words and make the sentence positive. Thus, The Rolling Stones really had nothing to complain about since if they couldn't get any satisfaction, then they could get some satisfaction. Right?

If a sentence below does not have a double negative problem, do nothing. But, if it does have a double negative problem, circle the letter found in parentheses before the sentence. Then write that letter in the space below the last sentence. Unscramble the letters you have written to form a word that can be placed in front of the words _____ parachute, _____ calf, and _____ cow.

1. (g)   I haven't done nothing well today.

2. (h)   Terry has to go to the store for she needs more allergy pills.

3. (l)   Nothing seems to make no difference to the leaders.

4. (a)   Herbert hasn't forgotten anything you taught him.

5. (s)   It doesn't seem to be a big deal to them.

6. (o)   We haven't located nothing in these reference books.

7. (u)   The hikers haven't found anything valuable to bring back with them.

8. (d)   Louise and Sean don't need no help.

9. (m)   They have only three weeks to complete the project.

10. (n)   This certainly makes no difference to me.

11. (e)   Lester has not seen no new magazines.

12. (n)   We don't need no education.

The letters in parentheses before the double negative sentences are _____

The word that can be placed in front of the words parachute, calf, and cow is _____.

45. CAPITAL LETTERS

Circle the words that require capital letters. If you have circled the correct words, a pattern has emerged. Can you identify the pattern of words requiring capital letters? Be ready to justify why you capitalized the words.

1. Last summer Abby visited two American cities, Tempe, arizona, and boston, Massachusetts.

2. When he returned from his trip, he called congressman david Jackson to ask him about the pollution issue.

3. eagerly awaiting Jackson's return call, Abby could hardly study for his french exam.

4. Abby also wanted to ask the politician about the grand Canyon and hoover Dam, two scenic tourist attractions.

5. Jackson returned Abby's call and spoke to him about indian affairs in the West.

6. justifying his votes on these controversial issues, Jackson said he had also spoken to other senators, including one from kentucky.

7. During two parts of the trip, Abby had flown on American Airlines with his lithuanian friend, mr. Richard Storm.

8. nearly fifty tourists had boarded another plane near omaha.

9. One of the passengers talked incessantly about her Junior prom.

10. One tourist, Ms. Adrienne q. Perry, said she knew much about the French revolution and the Bastille.

11. Another group of tourists Abby met said they had taken the train to Grand Central station in New York City and then walked to the Twin towers near Wall Street.

12. until he had gone on this trip, Abby did not fully realize how beautiful his country was.

13. During the trip he listened to his violent Femmes CD.

14. His walkman and some good tapes helped Abby get through some of the long afternoons.

15. Abby's social studies test next Wednesday would probably have questions on both xerxes, the historical figure, and an important meeting, the yalta Conference.

16. Perhaps there would even be a question on President zachary Taylor!

46. AN ABBREVIATED JOURNEY

This short story contains many abbreviations. Write each abbreviation's full word in the space provided after each abbreviation. The first one is done for you.

On Thurs. <u>Thursday</u>, Je _____ 29, the year 1950 A.D. _____,

Dr. _____ and Mrs._____ Steven Albright Sr. _____

left from their NY _____ home to drive to NJ _____. In only a

few secs. _____ they made a left out of Madison Rd. _____ and

headed for the tpke._____. Since the temperature was 75 degs._____,

Albright decided to roll down the car's windows. The couple had traveled about 10

km. _____ or 6.2 mi. _____ when they passed the

Rev. _____ Robt. _____ Arguilo's home and a building that had the

name Sanders Bros. _____ Inc. _____ written on its door.

Another store along the road was named Capt. _____ Elmer's.

Prof. _____ Watkins often ate at that rest. _____ which

had opened ten mos. _____ ago.

When 50 pct. _____ of the trip was completed, the Albrights, riding along at

55 m.p.h. _____, started to talk about Wash. _____, DC

_____ and the Lincoln Mem. _____. It would be exciting to

take the children along Penn. _____ Ave. _____ and then

to see the bldg. _____ called the Capitol. They would cruise the Potomac

Riv. _____ and stay in a fancy htl. _____. Perhaps they could

even talk to some sens. _____. They decided to do that trip

nxt. _____ yr. _____.

47. PERFECTING PUNCTUATION

Nine marks of punctuation are listed below. Each is displayed within brackets. Insert the proper punctuation mark next to the numbered spaces provided within each sentence. Be ready to explain why you used the punctuation mark in that space.

colon [:]	exclamation point [!]	question mark [?]
comma [,]	parentheses [( )]	quotation marks [" "]
dash [—]	period [.]	semicolon [;]

A. Pedro Alvarez (1) who won the senior class election for president, will be making some changes in our school (2)

B. What a great victory that was (3)

C. Ms (4) Kenorra believes Pedro will be an outstanding leader (5)

D. (6) Did the other teachers think Pedro would win by such a large margin (7) (8) asked Dr (9) Plorew (10)

E. The Alvarez family was ecstatic because of Pedro's victory (11) they planned a surprise celebration in his honor (12)

F. They will party at The Seascape Restaurant at 5 (13) 30 next Friday (14) October 4 (15)

G. The celebration (16) hardly a small affair (17) will be attended by more than one hundred people (18)

H. Ms (19) Yearwood (20) our school's principal (21) congratulated all the new senior class officers during the celebration (22)

I. When Pedro arrived at the restaurant (23) he was both shocked and happy (24)

J. He was so surprised (25) Pedro is not one to hide his emotions (26) that he could not speak for a few seconds (27)

K. Yes (28) the evening was a joyous occasion for the family and friends of Pedro Alvarez (29)

L. Pedro will do a good job as our leader (30)

© 1998 by John Wiley & Sons, Inc

48. SOMETHING'S UP WITH SIXTY-SEVEN

Some of these sentences contain mistakes in spelling, grammar, or usage. Some don't have any problems. If you add the numbers of the sentences that are correct, you will total 67. In the spaces before the sentences containing errors, write the correction. If the sentence has no errors, write a C in the appropriate space.

1. _____ There ain't no way that Fran and I can make it to the concert by ten o'clock.

2. _____ I think I will give my tickets to Laurine and he.

3. _____ We bought those tickets from Kyle last month.

4. _____ Kyle is the most funniest person I know.

5. _____ He can make anybody laugh when he puts his mind to it.

6. _____ Due you plan to take a bus or a train to get to the concert?

7. _____ The bus will leave the terminal about two hours before the start of the concert.

8. _____ The first rock group will perform for about an hour.

9. _____ Have you seen those musicians play at another concert?

10. _____ Last summer the featured group played a terrific concert in Toronto.

11. _____ Their latest CD has six of their new songs on it.

12. _____ Either Music Central or The Sensational Sound carry this CD.

13. _____ You might find information about the group when you go to the libary.

14. _____ Call me tomorrow morning and tell me if you liked the concert.

15. _____ Since I might not be home, leave a massage on my answering machine.

49. I CAN'T GET NOTHING RIGHT TODAY!

The person who composed these fifteen sentences below made a mistake in each sentence. Even the title of this exercise is incorrect. "I Can't Get Anything Right Today!" or "I Can Get Nothing Right Today!" are two correct ways to write the title. Correct the mistake in each sentence by writing the correction in the space provided next to each sentence.

1. _____ All the class officers accept Ben will attend the meeting.

2. _____ This year less students will be going to the ceremony.

3. _____ Luke will drive to the museum by hisself.

4. _____ Marcia acts quite respectively when she is in the company of adults.

5. _____ None of the team members had swam in that lake before today.

6. _____ We have little information concerning the amount of teens attending the review classes.

7. _____ He tends to speak soft whenever he is in a crowd.

8. _____ My best friend sings very good.

9. _____ We received the bad news that the CD player had busted when it was shipped by airplane.

10. _____ The delicious candy had been divided between the four of us.

11. _____ Nobody is as tall as him.

12. _____ I read where a wealthy man had made a large donation to a shelter for the homeless.

13. _____ Several of the baked goods was missing from the basket.

14. _____ Every one of the seventeen policemen have at least two uniforms.

15. _____ Nicole could of done the entire assignment in an hour.

© 1998 by John Wiley & Sons, Inc

50. USAGE CROSSWORD PUZZLE

Fill in the answers to these questions dealing with usage.

ACROSS

1. group of words that expresses a complete thought

4. predicate nominative in the sentence, Jack is the dean.

6. object of the preposition in the sentence, They went to the game.

8. Is allusion or illusion the noun meaning a reference to something?

10. helping verb in the sentence, They have gone into your tent.

11. possessive case form of the pronoun who

12. one sentence running on into another

13. verb tense in the sentence, You drove to the store.

17. verb tense in the sentence, I shall run with you.

20. group of words that does not express a complete thought

22. past tense of the verb drink

24. Which means full of respect—respectfully or respectively?

25. The three degrees of comparison of adjectives and adverbs are the positive, comparative and _____.

DOWN

1. Which means to place something down—set or sit?

2. preposition in the sentence, Hank fell near that tall pine tree.

3. committee, flock, group and jury are examples of this type of noun

5. part of speech of the word badly in the sentence, The band played badly.

6. Which one means valid or genuine—good or well?

7. past participle of the verb bear

8. type of voice for a verb expressing an action performed by its subject

9. past participle of the verb spring

10. reflexive pronoun in the sentence, Stephen brought himself to my father's mansion.

11. objective case form of the pronoun who

14. Is affect or effect always a verb?

15. part of speech of the word walking in the sentence Walking into the room, Bob felt uneasy.

16. Which is an adverb—than or then?

18. third person plural nominative case pronoun

19. past participle of the verb ride

21. Is accept or except the verb meaning to receive willingly?

22. singular form of the noun data

51. USAGE PRETEST

Here are twenty-five questions dealing with usage. These questions are similar to the ones you will see on the Final Usage Test. Write the correct answer in the appropriate space.

For the first four questions, indicate whether each group of words is a fragment (F), run-on (RU), or complete sentence (CS).

1. _____ Each of the girls from Detroit.

2. _____ None of the three teams will be there.

3. _____ Wandering in the valley after the setting of the sun.

4. _____ Jesse was campaigning for his brother-in-law, the effort was successful.

5. _____ Everyone in these classes (are, is) happy with the results.

6. _____ All of the breads (was, were) tasty.

7. _____ Most of the test questions (was, were) easy to solve.

8. _____ *The Three Musketeers* (are, is) his favorite book.

9. _____ The reasons for this accident (are, is) interesting.

10. _____ (Has, Have) Bernardo and she visited you lately?

11. _____ Have you seen the principal or (her, she)?

12. _____ I'll send the message to both you and (them, they).

13. _____ The famous actor, (who, whom) I read about, will be on stage today.

14. _____ Kendall Jones is an artist, (who, whom) I think will become famous very soon.

15. _____ Henry did the work by (himself, hisself).

16. _____ Leroy is not as friendly as (her, she).

17. _____ Ophelia did not like (you, your) screaming during the argument.

18. _____ She had (tore, torn) the poster by mistake.

19. _____ Before we knew it, spring had (sprang, sprung).

20. _____ The water level had been (raising, rising) throughout the night.

21. _____ Brett should (have, of) thought of that long before now.

22. _____ Everybody attending the Moving Up Dance felt (happily, happy).

23. _____ Most of the people felt (terrible, terribly) about what had happened there.

24. _____ Of the fifty people applying for the position, Sheila is the (more, most) qualified.

25. _____ Needless to say, Michael Jordan could (have, of) broken the scoring record.

Name _____ Date _____ Period _____

Score _____ %

52. FINAL TEST ON USAGE

Each correct answer is worth four points. Write the correct answer for each question in the space provided. Good luck!

Choices are given in parentheses for questions 5–25. For each of the first four questions, tell whether the group of words is a fragment (F), run-on (RU), or complete sentence (CS).

1. _____ Nothing could be better than this!

2. _____ Near the first turn during the championship race.

3. _____ Ask me later.

4. _____ The crowd filled the arena, then the band came out on the stage.

5. _____ Each of these four applicants (are, is) qualified.

6. _____ (Has, Have) all the contestants been interviewed?

7. _____ Joel, along with his classmates, (was, were) on the bus.

8. _____ Neither of the assignments (seem, seems) that difficult.

9. _____ (Doesn't, Don't) this dress fit well?

10. _____ Here (are, is) your brother and sister.

11. _____ Sixty dollars (are, is) the cost of the prom ticket.

12. _____ Mumps (are, is) a childhood illness.

13. _____ The finest present (was, were) the jewels you gave me for my birthday.

14. _____ It really (don't, doesn't) matter that much to me.

15. _____ Neither Ollie nor his sisters (are, is) able to attend the wedding.

16. _____ Here is one of the films that (was, were) taken out by your sister.

17. _____ Bradley is older than (I, me).

18. _____ The award was given to Paul and (her, she).

19. _____ To (who, whom) were you waving?

20. _____ The former coach, (who, whom) we will invite to the banquet, is nearly seventy years old.

21. _____ The minister and (I, me) will be going to the important meeting tonight.

22. _____ Wendy has already (driven, drove) forty miles.

23. _____ I wish I (was, were) taller.

24. _____ Mollie works very (good, well) with her teammates.

25. _____ Please (bring, take) this note to your neighbor.

Number of correct answers _____ × 4 = _____ % (Final Score)

53. IS IT OCTOPUSES OR OCTOPI?

If you have more than one octopus, do you have two octopuses or two octopi? Actually, the more accepted form is octopuses, though octopi is also correct. Here are twenty-five more words for you to pluralize. Write the correct form in the Plural Column.

SINGULAR COLUMN	PLURAL COLUMN
1. child	_____
2. church	_____
3. basis	_____
4. salmon	_____
5. cupful	_____
6. Smith	_____
7. woman	_____
8. criterion	_____
9. brother-in-law	_____
10. tomato	_____
11. embryo	_____
12. leaf	_____
13. passerby	_____
14. summary	_____
15. box	_____
16. medium	_____
17. beau	_____
18. oasis	_____
19. donkey	_____
20. index	_____
21. life	_____
22. veto	_____
23. 7	_____
24. radio	_____
25. t	_____

54. MAKING THEM ALL AGREE!

This activity tests your ability to make subjects and verbs agree. Circle the sentence's correct verb and then write the number above it in the space after the sentence. If you have selected the correct verbs, each group's total will be 9.

Group 1

1. Neither the girls nor their brother (is¹, are²) going to the show tonight. (   )

2. All of the beads (is¹, are²) missing. (   )

3. One of them (was³, were⁴) working in the museum. (   )

4. The lights in the basement (need¹, needs²) to be replaced soon. (   )

5. Todd, as well as the other players, (know¹, knows²) the award winner. (   )

Is the total 9? _____

Group 2

1. The paintings for this show (seem², seems³) to be better. (   )

2. Not one of the judges (has², have³) been pleased with the new rules. (   )

3. The heating in the older homes (is¹, are²) inadequate. (   )

4. Everyone in these classes (believe², believes³) that your story is more exciting. (   )

5. You (is², are¹) the one selected to represent us. (   )

Is the total 9? _____

Group 3

1. (Was¹, Were²) either of the paintings good? (   )

2. Both the team and the coaches (is², are¹) taking the seven o'clock plane tomorrow morning. (   )

3. Apples and oranges (has¹, have²) been part of my diet. (   )

4. (Does³, Do⁴) either of the girls need more confidence? (   )

5. Some of the cars (require², requires³) maintenance. (   )

Is the total 9? _____

55. FINAL TEST ON AGREEMENT

Circle the correct word in each sentence and then write it in the appropriate space next to the question's number. Each answer is worth five points. Good luck!

1. _____ The new driver's skillful use of hand signals (was, were) obvious.

2. _____ Consideration for other motorists and cyclists (are, is) a major concern for all drivers.

3. _____ An inexperienced driver, like all the other drivers, (are, is) responsible for many things while driving.

4. _____ Neither the policeman nor the pedestrians (was, were) able to give information about the stolen car.

5. _____ One of the shoppers (didn't, don't) see the car as it was being driven away.

6. _____ The police captain, along with several other officers, (was, were) able to gather some information about the car from its owner.

7. _____ Each of the six other policemen (has, have) been part of an investigation similar to this one.

8. _____ There (are, is) three other possible witnesses the police can call.

9. _____ The area they will examine (are, is) at the intersection of Mansfield Dr. and Seaman Neck Road.

10. _____ Three-fourths of the stolen cars (has, have) been found within two weeks.

11. _____ The police tactics in a situation like this one (are, is) interesting.

12. _____ After three hours the three culprits (was, were) apprehended.

13. _____ One of the three men who (was, were) later arrested was Frank's neighbor.

14. _____ "(Is, Are) there any other men involved in this robbery?" asked Frank.

15. _____ "Either these three men or a friend of theirs (are, is) the heart and soul behind this whole scheme," responded the police captain.

16. _____ Criminals like this ring leader (is, are) trouble to others.

17. _____ Neither the newspaper reporter nor her secretary (was, were) able to answer our questions.

18. _____ All of this information (are, is) hard to track down.

19. _____ Only one of the bits of information (make, makes) sense to us.

20. _____ Every one of our city's five newspapers (need, needs) to give full attention to this unfortunate event.

Number of correct answers _____ × 5 = _____%

Section Three

VOCABULARY

56. KNOWING THOSE ROOTS AND PREFIXES

These fifteen roots and prefixes in Column A should be matched with their meanings in Column B. If done correctly, the letters in Column B will spell out something quite interesting. Write the correct answers (each has a four-letter combination) in the spaces next to the numbers and then again below the last question. We have intentionally left all the letters in lower case. (Hint: No need to pray; you'll do okay!)

Column A		Column B	
1. _____ anti-		aism.	ten
2. _____ bene-		anca.	four
3. _____ deca-		elig.	insufficient
4. _____ dis-		esta.	all
5. _____ inter-		icwo.	across
6. _____ micro-		ions.	one
7. _____ neo-		isla.	against
8. _____ omni-		mjud.	kindly, good
9. _____ para-		mrom.	many
10. _____ poly-		ntis.	beside, beyond
11. _____ quadr-		oism.	small
12. _____ semi-		prot.	new
13. _____ trans-		rldr.	three
14. _____ tri-		shin.	not
15. _____ under-		thol.	half
16. _____ uni-		tota.	between, among

The 4-letter combinations in front of each answer spell out the following:

_____

_____ .

57. PREFIXES AND BASES

Sixteen prefixes and bases are listed in Column B. Place the letter of the matching prefix or base in the blank in front of the number in Column A.

Column A		Column B	
_____	1. NON-	A.	sym-
_____	2. BI-	B.	magn-
_____	3. SYN-	C.	tetra-
_____	4. UNI-	D.	di-
_____	5. MULTI-	E.	mod-
_____	6. DYS-	F.	bon-
_____	7. MES-	G.	im-
_____	8. LIB-	H.	arch-
_____	9. EU-	I.	punct-
_____	10. HYPER-	J.	mal-
_____	11. DIS-	K.	ex-
_____	12. SEMI-	L.	mono-
_____	13. AB-	M.	dif-
_____	14. QUAD-	N.	hemi-
_____	15. PRIM-	O.	biblio-
_____	16. PUNG-	P.	ultra-

58. PREFIXES CROSSWORD

How well do you know prefixes? They can be very helpful when trying to figure out a word's meaning. This crossword puzzle features **only** prefixes. When you are finished with the puzzle, see if you can think of at least one word that displays each prefix's meaning.

ACROSS

2. blame
5. half
7. both
9. speech
10. not
11. to bend
12. two
14. eight
17. new
18. across
20. backward
21. around
22. after
24. around
28. equal
29. hand
31. water
33. four
35. before
36. running

DOWN

1. again
2. time
3. many
4. beyond
5. under
6. between
7. against
8. life
13. inward
15. to believe
16. forward
18. three
19. name
21. five
22. before
23. to follow
25. against
26. bad
27. to step
28. love
29. big
30. over
31. six
32. hard
34. ten

59. ROOTS AND PREFIXES

Match these twenty roots and prefixes in Column A with their meanings. Write the letter of the matching definition from Column B in the space after the number in Column A.

Column A	Column B
1. _____ lex-	A. life
2. _____ culpa-	B. ship
3. _____ facilis-	C. shade
4. _____ populus-	D. fault
5. _____ bios-	E. book
6. _____ liber-	F. hand
7. _____ sophia-	G. law
8. _____ sanctus-	H. people
9. _____ anima-	I. work
10. _____ opus-	J. easy
11. _____ domus-	K. house
12. _____ navis-	L. wisdom
13. _____ umbra-	M. water
14. _____ aqua-	N. silence
15. _____ gramma-	O. heat
16. _____ ego-	P. breath
17. _____ thermo-	Q. letter
18. _____ manus-	R. I
19. _____ tacitus-	S. holy
20. _____ locus-	T. place

60. LATIN AND GREEK STEMS

Here are twenty stems from Latin and Greek. Circle the stem's correct meaning. Then write the first letter of each correct answer (in order) on the line below the last question. If your answers are correct, you will have spelled out the words that eager shoppers love to hear.

1. Does *cant* mean sing, one, middle or lessen?

2. Does *dent* mean join, hang, tooth or death?

3. Does *mand* mean kill, throw, conquer or order?

4. Does *crat* mean rule, science, heat or cut?

5. Which stem means *happy*? pseudo, eu, soph or agr

6. *Phone* means which of these? break, move, sound or follow

7. *Farm*'s stem is philo, sequ, junct or agr?

8. Which stem's definition is *to break*? thermo, min, rupt or spir

9. Which does *geo* mean? call, breathe, earth or sea

10. *Mono* is a stem for one, name, read or middle?

11. The stem for *father* is meter, pater, med or fring.

12. The stem *term* means end, move, write.

13. Does *nom* mean name, heat, origin or world?

14. Which means *heat*? homo, thermo, pseudo or philo

15. A word that shows the stem for *write* is dismiss, inscribe, suicide or dental.

16. Which stem means the *study of*? mand, manu, logy or hydr

17. The stem that means *to speak* is loq, astro, graph or auto.

18. *Hand*'s stem is tele, sed, manu or vent.

19. The word that shows the stem for *look* is inspect, paternity, conspire or refund.

20. Does *mort* mean father, death, stand or hold?

21. Which stem means *sailor*? naut, fund, mit or vict

22. Which word shows the stem for *run*? collect, synonym, status or incur

23. The stem for *group* is greg, tact, pos or ped.

24. The stem for *water* is scrib, hydr, mono or pathos.

25. The stem *tact* means touch, water, fall or close.

The first letters from each correct answer spell out

© 1998 by John Wiley & Sons, Inc

61. SIX COMMON TYPES OF ANALOGIES

Each type of analogy is used three times in this activity. Write the appropriate letter next to the matching pair of words. When you are finished, you should have three answers for each of the six types of analogies. In the area below the last question, write your own example of each type of analogy. Share your answers with your classmates.

a. Synonym   c. Characteristic   e. Degree or intensity

b. Antonym   d. Part of   f. Type of

1. ____ stanza : poem   10. ____ happy : sad

2. ____ intelligence : scientist   11. ____ applaud : clap

3. ____ cirrus : cloud   12. ____ tall : gigantic

4. ____ haiku : poem   13. ____ detective : curiosity

5. ____ swift : fast   14. ____ elbow : arm

6. ____ cod : fish   15. ____ misdemeanor : felony

7. ____ gums : mouth   16. ____ truthful : honest

8. ____ shallow : deep   17. ____ small : minuscule

9. ____ clear : hazy   18. ____ cheetah : speed

Synonym: _____

Antonym: _____

Characteristic: _____

Part of: _____

Degree or intensity: _____

Type of: _____

62. ANALYZING ANALOGIES

Analogies show a relationship between two words. A typical analogy is **tree : forest**. The tree is part of the forest so the relationship would be written **part : whole**. Other common relationships are found in this exercise. Match the type of relationship in Column A with its example in Column B. If your answers are correct, the answers for letters A-F should total 39, the same number as the total for answers for letters G-L.

Column A	Column B
a. _____ synonyms	1. laugh : humor
b. _____ antonyms	2. library : book
c. _____ characteristic	3. old : new
d. _____ indication or sign of	4. car : vehicle
e. _____ degree or intensity	5. star : constellation
f. _____ place for	6. carpenter : hammer
g. _____ interruption	7. teen : adult
h. _____ part of	8. cardiologist : heart
i. _____ type of	9. oil : friction
j. _____ order or sequence	10. athlete : coordination
k. _____ tool	11. cold : freezing
l. _____ field of study	12. marry : wed

Name _____ Date _____ Period _____

63. AN ANALOGY CROSSWORD PUZZLE

Thirty-three analogies make up the questions for this crossword puzzle. Complete the analogy by writing the missing word in its appropriate place within the crossword puzzle.

ACROSS

1. arson : crime as rose : _____
3. judge : courtroom as teacher : _____
5. star : _____ as island : archipelago
9. raze : demolish as raise : _____
13. historian : past as _____ : future
15. closely : _____ as architect : noun
17. affluent : _____ as indigent : poor
18. man : boy as woman : _____
22. dolphin : ocean as camel : _____
23. wrist : elbow as _____ : knee
24. _____ : stale as old : new
26. meteorologist : _____ as botanist : plants
27. sentences : _____ as scenes : act
29. Ottawa : _____ as London : England
30. beneficent : good as _____ : evil
31. dolt : stupid as genius : _____

DOWN

2. work : _____ as relax : rest
4. peninsula : _____ as inlet : water
6. horse : terrestrial as whale : _____
7. poem : _____ as novel : chapter
8. cardiac : _____ as vascular : vein
10. soliloquy : drama as aria : _____
11. _____ : tree as torso : human
12. _____ : hot as frigid : cold
13. _____ : guitar as bow : cello
14. lion : den as bee : _____
15. bring : verb as tall : _____
16. _____ : end as alpha : omega
19. ruler : _____ as watch : time
20. consecrate : bless as _____ : profane
21. king : queen as duke : _____
25. _____ : page as border : country
28. _____ : contractor as commission : painter

67

64. MAKING UP YOUR OWN ANALOGIES

Each of the words that you will use in making up analogies in this activity has at least two or more definitions. As an example, in some dictionaries the word **run** has over one hundred definitions. Thus, if you wrote **run : baseball, run : stocking** or **run : office**, you have shown three different meanings of the word **run**. In the spaces below, complete the analogy for each word having two or more meanings. In the space after the analogy, explain the relationship. The first question is done for you.

1. set :   tennis   A set is a group of six or more games won in the game of tennis.

2. set : _____   _____

3. set : _____   _____

4. school : _____   _____

5. school : _____   _____

6. strip : _____   _____

7. strip : _____   _____

8. level : _____   _____

9. level : _____   _____

10. cast : _____   _____

11. cast : _____   _____

12. charge : _____   _____

13. charge : _____   _____

14. cross : _____   _____

15. cross : _____   _____

16. square : _____   _____

17. square : _____   _____

18. seal : _____   _____

19. seal : _____   _____

20. seal : _____   _____

© 1998 by John Wiley & Sons, Inc

65. ADJECTIVES FROM A TO Z

This puzzle features an adjective for every letter of the alphabet. The twenty-six adjectives are placed backwards, forward, diagonally, and up and down. The first letters of the adjectives are listed below. The number after the space indicates the number of letters in the adjective. Write each adjective in its proper place.

```
I  T  Y  B  W  H  T  M  Y  M  J  S  L  N  H  F  G  F  D  K  F  G  J  Z
N  R  B  T  N  S  E  N  M  H  V  N  A  T  F  L  D  L  R  B  I  O  K  P
T  E  P  B  Z  V  N  D  I  E  G  Y  U  L  F  A  C  D  A  D  V  N  L  K
E  M  Z  T  A  X  Q  V  Z  A  N  Y  S  R  I  G  I  D  M  I  L  D  D  X
L  E  H  R  K  M  I  M  S  V  U  S  U  H  L  R  B  M  A  D  A  I  I  P
L  N  B  Y  P  C  B  T  L  Y  E  Q  B  E  Q  A  O  L  T  N  N  C  L  C
I  D  M  C  I  E  U  U  F  L  K  Z  E  K  Y  N  H  Q  I  A  O  A  O  M
G  O  L  O  W  T  F  Q  E  Z  B  F  Y  X  H  T  P  M  C  C  I  L  S  Z
E  U  U  H  E  H  Y  F  J  Y  U  J  T  X  W  M  O  H  G  B  T  P  J  C
N  S  F  S  T  K  I  H  I  L  Q  V  H  R  D  Z  N  M  C  N  P  X  R  B
T  V  E  U  T  L  G  W  H  C  D  F  G  K  F  J  E  N  N  C  O  P  Y  Z
W  N  O  N  C  B  C  L  C  N  I  T  U  T  P  Z  X  H  Q  Y  P  L  P  D
T  Y  W  L  Q  H  T  X  M  P  Z  E  A  W  F  L  L  K  J  M  M  L  X  W
B  Q  V  K  N  R  T  G  J  T  L  G  N  H  B  T  G  H  Z  X  S  R  C  V
V  P  P  L  V  G  J  S  L  B  M  Z  X  T  D  D  W  X  T  W  D  N  K  C
P  D  S  V  G  P  Q  Z  T  M  L  B  P  L  V  H  W  F  J  Z  R  C  N  N
Z  M  G  L  L  S  W  D  Q  P  T  B  W  F  Q  V  S  Y  N  P  R  Z  T  G
```

A _____ (6)   K _____ (4)   U _____ (5)

B _____ (5)   L _____ (8)   V _____ (7)

C _____ (6)   M _____ (4)   W _____ (6)

D _____ (8)   N _____ (7)   X _____ (10)

E _____ (9)   O _____ (8)   Y _____ (8)

F _____ (8)   P _____ (6)   Z _____ (4)

G _____ (7)   Q _____ (6)

H _____ (5)   R _____ (5)

I _____ (11)   S _____ (5)

J _____ (6)   T _____ (10)

66. VOCABULARY AND ADJECTIVES

This activity will improve both your vocabulary and your creativity. In the blank spaces, write a word that begins with the letter in that space. All twenty-six letters of the alphabet have been used.

1. The a _____ senior citizen delivered the b_____ present to the family.

2. C_____ behavior will demand d_____ measures.

3. An e_____ grade will demand your f_____ effort.

4. G_____ advice and a h_____ welcome are his trademarks.

5. An i_____ way to approach the j_____ problem is to ask the k_____ man for his help.

6. This is our l_____ chance to see the m_____ actors before they travel to their n_____ location.

7. An o_____ child, Heather enjoyed the company of her p_____ friends.

8. The q_____ expression on her face told us that her r_____ position on the team was now in jeopardy.

9. With a s_____ look on his face, Sam approached the t_____ dog that was hiding in the u_____ room.

10. The area was coping with a v_____ blizzard.

11. We kept a w_____ eye on the newcomer since we were x_____ in nature.

12. The y_____ woman acted in a z_____ manner.

67. SELECTING THE RIGHT WORD FOR THE RIGHT PERSON

Fifteen adjectives to describe fifteen people are listed below. In the space before the sentence, write the best word to describe that person based on the action performed. Each word is used only once. The first one is done for you.

articulate	expressive	punctual
creative	honest	scholarly
devoted	indomitable	stable
diligent	inquisitive	unpretentious
empathetic	motivated	witty

1. ____witty____ Mariana is very funny.

2. _____ Stu speaks very well.

3. _____ Lori is always on time.

4. _____ Hector is candid.

5. _____ Ned is quite humble.

6. _____ Luke likes to ask questions.

7. _____ Gloria is dedicated.

8. _____ Isaac is able to share in another person's emotions.

9. _____ Pedro is a goal-oriented individual.

10. _____ Juan is very imaginative and artistic.

11. _____ Julie is studious.

12. _____ Drew shows his emotions quite readily and easily.

13. _____ Teresa is hard-working and industrious.

14. _____ Jim was emotionally steady in all situations.

15. _____ Tommy was not easily discouraged or defeated when it came to getting a summer job.

68. IS IT AS SIMPLE AS A, B, C OR D?

Who will win this contest? Will it be A, B, C or D? Place the letter of the term that matches the description in the blank in front of the number. When finished, count up the number of times each letter is the correct answer and write the results next to the letters after the last question. Then circle the winning letter.

_____ 1. urgency
    A. frugal   B. exigency   C. clique   D. mitigate

_____ 2. kind
    A. benign   B. agile   C. exigency   D. jocular

_____ 3. showing little emotion
    A. stymie   B. stoic   C. deference   D. succumb

_____ 4. gloomy
    A. clique   B. morose   C. stoic   D. mitigate

_____ 5. longing for sadly
    A. wistful   B. sycophant   C. agile   D. mitigate

_____ 6. flexible
    A. labyrinth   B. agile   C. sycophant   D. stoic

_____ 7. full of love
    A. amorous   B. benign   C. stymie   D. exigency

_____ 8. one who is servile to another
    A. sycophant   B. benign   C. labyrinth   D. yen

_____ 9. to thwart
    A. agile   B. labyrinth   C. stymie   D. jocular

_____ 10. maze
    A. labyrinth   B. jocular   C. wistful   D. covert

_____ 11. urge
    A. amorous   B. stymie   C. stoic   D. yen

_____ 12. humorous
    A. benign   B. jocular   C. yen   D. labyrinth

_____ 13. the outside
    A. agile   B. sycophant   C. yen   D. periphery

_____ 14. small, exclusive group of people
    A. covert   B. jocular   C. exigency   D. clique

_____ 15. hidden or secret
    A. mitigate   B. exigency   C. deference   D. covert

_____ 16. to moderate the effect
    A. peruse   B. stymie   C. stoic   D. mitigate

_____ 17. to examine carefully
    A. deference   B. peruse   C. wistful   D. morose

_____ 18. not spending much
    A. mitigate   B. yen   C. jocular   D. frugal

_____ 19. to yield to
    A. succumb   B. agile   C. deference   D. stymie

_____ 20. respect
    A. frugal   B. clique   C. stymie   D. deference

    A. _____   B. _____   C. _____   D._____

69. HOW MANY DIFFERENT WAYS CAN IT BE DONE?

How did you walk into class today? Did you shuffle? stride? pace? trudge? waddle? Perhaps you entered in your own unique style. As you can see, an action can be done in a number of ways and the good writer attempts to use the exact word to describe how something is done. Here is your chance to tell the difference between one action and another.

From the three groups of words, match the word with its definition and write the letter in the space next to the definition. If your answers are correct, you will find three words in your answer key. Write those words beneath the last question. Each letter is used only once.

Ways of talking: (l) chatter   (k) discuss   (h) gossip   (f) orate   (j) preach

Movements made by the mouth: (c) beam   (e) grimace   (m) grin   (a) smirk   (i) sneer

Ways of eating: (g) crunch   (o) devour   (d) dine   (n) nibble   (b) sup

1. _____ to smile warmly

2. _____ to engage in rumors

3. _____ to smile in a conceited way

4. _____ to take small bites

5. _____ to bite with a noisy sound

6. _____ to distort the face to express pain or disgust

7. _____ to smile in amusement

8. _____ to smile in a scornful manner

9. _____ to talk fast and incessantly

10. _____ to talk about in a deliberate fashion

11. _____ to give a sermon

12. _____ to eat up hungrily or greedily

13. _____ to eat an evening meal

14. _____ to speak in a pompous manner

15. _____ to provide a dinner for

The three words found in the answer key are _____, _____ and _____.

70. READING PEOPLE'S MOODS

A person's facial or body expressions or actions often indicate his or her mood(s). Using the facial or body expression/action given to you in each question, write the mood indicated by that movement. If there could be more than one mood for a particular expression/action, indicate the other mood(s). Be ready to justify your answer. The first one is done for you.

1. raising one's eyebrows _____disbelief, question, concern_____

2. yawning _____

3. sneering _____

4. smirking _____

5. giggling _____

6. chuckling _____

7. grimacing _____

8. sighing _____

9. leering _____

10. biting one's bottom lip _____

11. looking off into space _____

12. laughing softly and moving one's head back and forth horizontally _____

_____

13. glancing repeatedly at the classroom clock _____

_____

14. folding one's arms on the chest and looking sternly at another _____

_____

15. looking down after being scolded _____

71. WHEN IS A SMILE A GRIN? WHEN IS A LAUGH A GUFFAW?

When a writer comes up with an idea for a story, he or she will include appropriate diction (words) to convey the exact feeling, description or impression. Using the word **strutted** instead of **walked** and **chatted** instead of **talked** will help to give the reader a more exact picture of what is happening in the story.

Fifteen words are found in Column A. Write a more specific word for that word in Column B. The word's part of speech is indicated after the word. The first one is done for you.

Column A	Column B
1. throw (verb)	hurl, toss, fling
2. run (verb)	
3. damage (verb)	
4. cold (adjective)	
5. fight (noun)	
6. good (adjective)	
7. heavy (adjective)	
8. big (adjective)	
9. easy (adjective)	
10. ask (verb)	
11. bad (adjective)	
12. feel (verb)	
13. see (verb)	
14. nice (adjective)	
15. like (verb)	

72. WHY IS A SANDAL BETTER THAN THE OTHER TWO?

The activity's title could have used the words "Footwear" or "Shoe." Instead it uses "Sandal" because it is a more specific word and tells more exactly what one is wearing. Good writers look for the most exact word to describe a person, place or thing. In this activity you will work on being specific. Twenty general words are given in Column A. Write a more specific word in Column B and an even more specific word in Column C. Avoid brand names. The first question is answered for you.

Column A	Column B	Column C
1. furniture	chair	captain's chair
2. vehicle		
3. literature		
4. science		
5. road		
6. sport		
7. animal		
8. food		
9. music		
10. group		
11. musical instrument		
12. game		
13. merchandise		
14. human being		
15. clothing		
16. entertainment		
17. machine		
18. fruit		
19. emotion		
20. tool		

© 1998 by John Wiley & Sons, Inc

73. ODD ONE OUT

Each of the following groups of words contains a word that does not belong with the others. Circle that word and write the reason why it does not belong with the others on the line below each group. Then write the first letter of each correct answer on the line below the last question to spell a word that means odd.

1. concept   idea   belief   underpass   thought

_____

2. ascend   soar   uprise   negate   surmount

_____

3. sword   knife   foil   channel   dagger

_____

4. oblique   ornery   circuitous   roundabout   meandering

_____

5. falter   hesitate   nimble   waver   oscillate

_____

6. glorify   honor   veneer   exalt   worship

_____

7. curtail   embroil   decrease   retrench   diminish

_____

8. poise   composure   equilibrium   assurance   negligence

_____

9. start   embark   trample   commence   begin

_____

10. invade   bring   carry   convey   transport

_____

11. aid   help   assist   oust   abet

_____

12. notebook   diary   nonentity   chronicle   record

_____

13. jinx   aspire   curse   hex   spell

_____

14. tempt   allure   lag   entice   tantalize

_____

Write the first letters of the fourteen correct answers in order here: _____

74. THE NAME GAME

Since there are twenty-six vocabulary words, each beginning with a different letter of the alphabet, this activity will literally take you from A to Z. Match the word in Column A with its definition in Column B by writing the two-letter answer choice in the space next to the number. Then write the two-letter answer for each consecutive question in the space below the last question and the title of this activity starts to make sense.

Column A		Column B	
1. ___ austere		an.	horrible; ghostly pale
2. ___ brazen		as.	rural
3. ___ candid		be.	bold; impudent
4. ___ dregs		bo.	crazy
5. ___ eulogy		ci.	refuge
6. ___ fraudulent		fr.	fake
7. ___ ghastly		ha.	dull; lifeless
8. ___ haven		hn.	funeral speech
9. ___ inconsequential		ia.	sophisticated
10. ___ jovial		jo.	residue
11. ___ kindle		ka.	vague
12. ___ labyrinth		ky.	maze
13. ___ meander		le.	to wander
14. ___ nebulous		lo.	fear of foreigners
15. ___ opulent		lv.	lukewarm
16. ___ petulant		ma.	happy
17. ___ quixotic		ne.	trifling
18. ___ rustic		nk.	coax; cajole
19. ___ sane		om.	idealistic but impractical
20. ___ tepid		ra.	wealthy
21. ___ urbane		ri.	urge; Japanese coin
22. ___ vapid		rk.	to start
23. ___ wheedle		ro.	stern; strict; severe
24. ___ xenophobia		rt.	frank; open; sincere
25. ___ yen		sy.	sensible
26. ___ zany		th.	peevish; irritable

The letters are: _____

_____

How are these letters and the activity's title tied together?

_____

75. REVOLUTIONARY VOCABULARY

This activity will identify those who are into revolution. Match the vocabulary words in Column A with their definitions in Column B. Yes, each choice has an answer that is either three letters, as in *art*, or two letters and a number, as in *n9p*. When you are finished, the consecutive letters in your answers will spell out the names of these "revolutionaries." To find these names, write your answers in the space next to each number and then again in the space below the last question.

Column A		Column B	
1. ____ agenda		art.	animal with two feet
2. ____ antidote		enu.	not stated directly
3. ____ biped		ept.	wandering
4. ____ cliché		eru.	pleasant sound
5. ____ durable		ets.	to increase
6. ____ euphony		hju.	overused expression
7. ____ falter		lan.	final
8. ____ hydrophobia		mar.	scarcity
9. ____ implied		n9p.	short and to the point
10. ____ juxtapose		pit.	lasting
11. ____ lucid		plu.	schedule of a meeting
12. ____ monotony		ran.	to hesitate
13. ____ nomadic		rcu.	clear
14. ____ noxious		ryn.	sameness
15. ____ paucity		sme.	to place next to one another
16. ____ poise		ssa.	composure
17. ____ sober		toe.	remedy for a poison
18. ____ terse		tur.	serious; not drunk
19. ____ ultimate		une.	poisonous; harmful
20. ____ wax		usv.	fear of water

The revolutionaries are _____

_____

_____.

76. ALL IN THE FAMILY

Twenty nouns are listed in Column A. Write the adjective form of the word in Column B and the verb form of the word in Column C.

Column A (Nouns)	Column B (Adjectives)	Column C (Verbs)
1. deafness	_____	_____
2. annoyance	_____	_____
3. calmness	_____	_____
4. obsession	_____	_____
5. expiration	_____	_____
6. derivation	_____	_____
7. definition	_____	_____
8. narration	_____	_____
9. reformation	_____	_____
10. repulsion	_____	_____
11. attraction	_____	_____
12. enticement	_____	_____
13. rebellion	_____	_____
14. articulateness	_____	_____
15. commendation	_____	_____
16. acclamation	_____	_____
17. instruction	_____	_____
18. prolongation	_____	_____
19. restriction	_____	_____
20. tyranny	_____	_____

77. HE HAD GROWN THE _____ PLANTS

The missing word is one of the activity title's words with its letters rearranged. What word belongs in the blank? **Wrong** is the answer since the letters of **grown** can be rearranged to spell wrong. Fill in the blank within each sentence by rearranging one of the sentence's words.

1. She sewed the decal around the _____ portion of the banner.

2. He didn't like the remark Harold made about the _____.

3. Candy saw the large person _____ at her.

4. A good chef will tell you whether you should _____ the meats.

5. The explorer brought back _____ from his expedition to the East.

6. When he saw how badly his mantle had been damaged, he had to _____.

7. All of them attempted to put the _____ on Mabel.

8. Kyle showed that his singing talent was certainly _____.

9. Every Easter Eddie plays the part of the _____ with the little kids during the egg hunt.

10. There was quite a bit of _____ for the animals to roam on the moor.

11. I certainly hope that this paint did not _____ your satin dress.

12. The Mexican posse went searching for the stolen _____.

13. The majestic mountain _____ are attractions to speak about often.

14. Paula eventually found the _____ near the plates.

15. Was the priest talking about a _____ during his sermon today?

78. STANDARD WORDS FOR STANDARDIZED TESTS

Test your vocabulary skill with this crossword puzzle that features words often found on standardized tests. Also included within the puzzle are some questions dealing with celebrities and culture. Do your best to fill in all these spaces. Good luck.

ACROSS
1. star of "Rainman"
3. to reject
5. Canadian province
7. to worry
8. to reduce or lessen
9. to hate
12. kind; good; not harmful
13. former U.S. president
15. misery
16. Italy's capital city
18. short for Daniel
20. known to only a few
23. rock and roller Elvis
25. actor _____ Pitt
26. limber; flexible
29. *Green Eggs and* _____
30. found in a mouth and on a shoe
31. baker's dozen
32. *101* _____

DOWN
1. king who was a merry old soul
2. strict
4. having tiny holes
5. cable television station
6. to waste away, often from disease
7. to mock
8. frank; open; honest
9. skillful
10. weighty
11. out of date
14. to protect
15. where Alice went
17. easily bent
19. truth
21. Eskimo's home
22. baby kangaroo
23. irreverent
24. past tense of swim
27. former Canadian prime minister
28. ice sport

79. FOUR-LETTER WORD SCRAMBLE

Twenty-five four-letter words have been scrambled in Column B. Their definitions are in Column C. Unscramble and write the correct word in Column A and the letter in front of the correct definition in the space before the word. The first one is done for you.

Column A	Column B	Column C
1. _p_ aura	uraa	a. all alone
2. __ _____	tdaa	b. boyfriend
3. __ _____	aoht	c. eager
4. __ _____	ueba	d. enthusiasm
5. __ _____	diel	e. faction
6. __ _____	sjet	f. facts
7. __ _____	dilo	g. joke
8. __ _____	iste	h. main idea
9. __ _____	scet	i. not busy
10. __ _____	iehr	j. one who inherits
11. __ _____	uped	k. pile
12. __ _____	diov	l. position or place
13. __ _____	avin	m. promise
14. __ _____	yolw	n. person worshipped
15. __ _____	hneo	o. request
16. __ _____	sleo	p. atmosphere
17. __ _____	hpea	q. to deceive
18. __ _____	eict	r. to declare openly
19. __ _____	lnae	s. to invalidate
20. __ _____	vaow	t. to quote
21. __ _____	vaid	u. to sharpen
22. __ _____	oram	v. to wander
23. __ _____	elpa	w. type of gas
24. __ _____	sgit	x. unsuccessful
25. __ _____	neno	y. wailing cry

80. ONOMATOPOEIA—WORDS WITH SOME SMASH!

Snap, **crackle** and **pop** are three words that are examples of the literary term onomatopoeia. Such words sound like what they mean. Thirty other examples of onomatopoeia are found within this puzzle. The words are placed backwards, forward, diagonally, and up and down. Circle them and write each word in its appropriate space below the puzzle. The number following each space indicates the number of letters in the word.

```
D C Q M B Z F M W M Y W Q P P G Z J G B D T S G
F Y K L T H F G B Y G R B D M P Y X T C L Q P H
H J Y N Z K C S P J P C C P W V J F C X P V J S
M S N L S L M V L M M P Z L J S H L N V Z Q N Y
Y K W S B J K P N G K N H J I X Z L P X K Z K W
G M H K P V C Z P C R K Z Z W S K T H G R C P S
X N A Q P L I X U S Q G Z B N M F R K O A N R B
Q N C J J S L L Y M P L N Q P B O A H U O N H H
Z Q K N I L C Z X K E Z O O M G R O Q N Z T K V
B X F P L L N R S R Z O P J B W N R X Z Z C K B
B O Q P A K P V A I P B W P G K H A U D A L S S
C H O C C G F L F T S Q A N N H S B L R J C C M
N R K M H P L X O Q C P X N J I L M C C R I N G
B M R Z M Z X P U P L H L Y G S R K A E M B G B
T R N U N M Z I P Z D Z S A F S N S E S B J G J
R J H R K P S X N R N D D M T H C C J R H R R G
V T G N D H M J V Y H W T B J H H J P S C R Z F
```

B_____ (4)	F _____ (4)	R _____ (4)
B_____ (4)	H _____ (4)	S _____ (7)
B_____ (4)	H _____ (4)	S _____ (7)
B_____ (4)	H _____ (4)	S _____ (6)
C_____ (5)	M _____ (4)	S _____ (5)
C_____ (5)	M _____ (3)	S _____ (5)
C_____ (5)	P _____ (4)	S _____ (6)
C_____ (5)	P _____ (3)	T _____ (5)
C_____ (5)	Q _____ (5)	W _____ (5)
C_____ (5)	R _____ (4)	Z _____ (4)

© 1998 by John Wiley & Sons, Inc

81. THE XYZ AFFAIR

History tells of the XYZ Affair, the 1797 incident involving French agents known simply as X, Y, and Z. Here is another XYZ Affair. Only words that begin with the letters x, y, or z are the correct answers to this puzzle's clues. See if the XYZ Affair is as easy as ABC! Good luck!

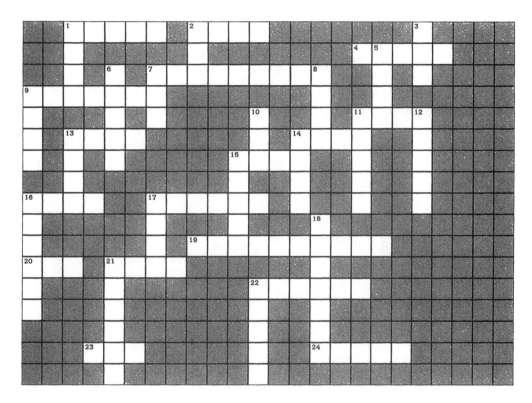

ACROSS

1. device for copying printed material
2. thirty-six inches
4. the woody, vascular tissue of a plant
7. the day before today
9. Jewish school
11. band of electromagnetic radiation
13. an egg's substance
14. area
15. system of exercise
16. iron's protective coating
17. it has its signs
19. fear or hatred of strangers
20. ____ Code
21. type of lens or camera shot
22. a color
23. type of tree
24. very tasty

DOWN

1. a variation of the word Christmas
2. opposite of no
3. Japanese coin
5. twelve months
6. give in to
7. an ox
8. child's toy
9. used for weaving
10. collection of wild animals
11. a colorless, noble, gaseous chemical element
12. relatively small sea vessel
13. exhibit tiredness
14. very foolish
15. long for
16. type of pattern
17. nothing
18. science dealing with animals
21. an instrument
22. leaven

82. PUTTING THE PIECES TOGETHER

The letters of fifteen words have been separated and placed into the three rows below. These letters appear in the order that they appear in the word itself. Thus taking the **ac** from Row 1, the **cur** from Row 2, and the **ate** from Row 3, you have spelled the word **accurate**. Each of the forty-five letter combinations is used once only. Write the fifteen words in the spaces below Row 3.

Row 1: ~~ac~~ corr fo fra go gr hy lab me re sop su ty who wr

Row 2: a br ce ct ~~cur~~ el es hom les or ra re ssa sse ue

Row 3: ~~ate~~ ative atory id ign ion ive mer nger nny ome ore some tle ve

_____   _____   _____

_____   _____   _____

_____   _____   _____

_____   _____   _____

_____   _____   _____

Name _____ Date _____ Period _____

83. YOU *CAN* DO THIS!

Every answer to this puzzle starts with the three letters *can*. Fill in the correct answers and enjoy!

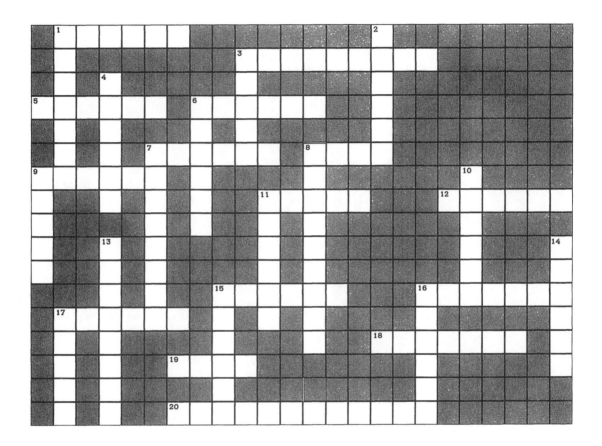

ACROSS	DOWN
1. false report with wicked intentions	1. card game
3. one running for office	2. waxy burner
5. small, yellow bird	3. narrow, light boat
6. open, honest, sincere	4. lively dance
7. disease	6. annul
8. walking stick	7. Australia's capital
9. country above the U.S.A.	8. type of bowling
11. sweets	9. artificial waterway
12. French Canadian	10. Chinese city
15. awning	11. dog or tooth
16. flask	13. person who eats human flesh
17. tent's fabric	14. narrow, long valley situated between cliffs
18. solicit	15. large piece of artillery
19. jargon	16. church choir leader
20. hospital helper	17. shrewd

84. WHEN ONE LETTER FOLLOWS THE OTHER

The word **clad**, meaning dressed, starts with the letter **c** and ends with the letter **d**. Thus, the word's first letter directly precedes the word's last letter as they appear in the alphabet. Fifteen words whose first and last letter patterns follow the first and last letter pattern of the word **clad** can be found in this puzzle. Circle the words and write them next to their definitions which appear below the puzzle. Words are placed backwards, forward, diagonally, and up and down.

```
L K Y D L N Q Q S B F Q P Y C V C G T M Q F H X
F Y W W Y S Z B N Z H M Y K S L V V Q M X X S L
F D X Z B Y J M L W M W B K N G K D X X O Q D X
V K L H T C K C Q B D J M G D P B Y Z W S O U V
S C N F M T Q V S D Z R R Z R F W X Q K X G N W
R T Y B S C J V T B R D T W P O L B M J A Z C L
Z Y A E V Y V X I F C D R W J Z W G C L J Q E V
L T L R W T L V M E Z L W N C M L T F T A H P T
K O G Y T S B B W Y W K R I L L W L H O C T R G
R B O H B M A P H A N Q X B Q L B H G F K E D S
N T X M N H R L X F H W X J X J C T W U E G X R
Q G Q S A L Z F N Z F S R R C R R R G U L K G B
C L A D D Z P V R L J V N L P N K P Q M V D V X
T M G Y N M T H Q F Y M L N M J Y R Q C G F Z D
N J F C L F G F T N S T M W B S F H H M W D S F
C Y X K T P L F W Y Y D G W Y R B G X W C K Z K
K X N W S D D S W B H M R B G H M Q N Q N D H K
```

a celestial body(4) _____   odd(5) _____
a cheeselike food high in   parts in a play(5)_____
   protein(4) _____   sight or vision(4) _____
a famous captain(4) _____   the main food of whalebone
a machine for weaving   whales(5) _____
   thread(4) _____   the process of developing(6) _____
a piece of cloth(4) _____   to increase(3)_____
a stupid person(5)_____   tool found in the car's
commence(5) _____   trunk(4) _____
dressed(4)_____

© 1998 by John Wiley & Sons, Inc

85. WHAT FOLLOWS WAR

The title of this activity may lead you to think this is a page of Social Studies questions or topics. It is really an activity that asks you to think of twenty words that begin with the letters *war*. The definitions for these twenty words that begin with war are found below the crossword. Fill in the correct words all beginning with *war*.

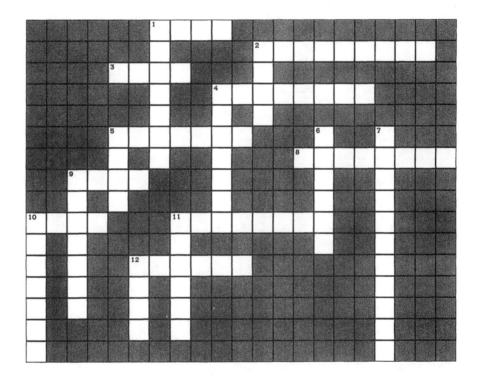

ACROSS	**DOWN**
1. caution	1. an aggressive tyrant
2. a building where goods are stored	2. pottery
3. to bend	4. soldier
4. guardianship	5. not cold
5. the act of waging war	6. space where rabbits breed
8. guarantee, especially on a product	7. sympathetic and kind
9. small, hard growth on the skin	9. a person who practices black magic
10. cautious	10. to authorize or sanction
11. a room where clothes are kept	11. a prison official
12. to make a musical sound	12. a section of a hospital

86. DON'T BE FACETIOUS! IT'S TIME TO THINK ABOUT WORDS!

The word **facetious** is interesting in that it contains all five vowels in the same order that they appear in the alphabet (f**a**c**e**t**iou**s). This activity features questions that will make you think about words and their construction. Write your answers in the spaces provided. Have fun!

1. Besides facetious, name another word that contains all five vowels in the same order that they appear in the alphabet. _____

2. Name three words that begin with the silent letter **p**.

   _____ _____ _____

3. Name three words that start with the letter **c** but sound as though they start with the letter **k**.

   _____ _____ _____

4. List four words that show how the letter combination "**ough**" has four different sounds.

   _____ _____ _____ _____

5. Without using plurals, name a word of five or more letters whose only vowel is the letter **a**. _____

6. Without using plurals, name a word of five or more letters whose only vowel is the letter **e**. _____

7. Without using plurals, name a word of five or more letters whose only vowel is the letter **i**. _____

8. Without using plurals, name a word of five or more letters whose only vowel is the letter **o**. _____

9. Without using vowels, name a word of five or more letters whose only vowel, the letter **u**, appears twice. _____

10. What is a word that contains an **aa** combination? _____

11. What is a word that contains an **ee** combination? _____

12. What is a word that contains an **ii** combination? _____

13. What is a word that contains an **oo** combination? _____

14. What is a word that contains a **uu** combination? _____

87. EUPHEMISMS

A euphemism is a word or phrase that is both less direct and less offensive at the same time. Using the expression, "He met his Maker," instead of, "He croaked," we express death in a less distasteful manner. Match the euphemisms in Column A with their more offensive equivalents in Column B.

Column A

1. _____ abdomen

2. _____ die

3. _____ dysfunctional

4. _____ expectorate

5. _____ indifferent

6. _____ intoxicated

7. _____ mortician

8. _____ officer of the law

9. _____ perpetrator

10. _____ perspire

11. _____ plagiarize

12. _____ prevaricate

13. _____ remains

14. _____ vertically challenged

15. _____ vomit

Column B

a. cheat

b. cop

c. corpse

d. couldn't care less

e. criminal

f. drunk

g. kick the bucket

h. lie

i. messed up

j. short

k. spit

l. stomach

m. sweat

n. undertaker

o. upchuck

Section Four

MECHANICS & WORD PLAY

Name _____ Date _____ Period _____

88. LEARNING FROM THE GRATE DEPRESSION

While reading the activity's title, you probably looked twice. Yes, the word **grate** is spelled incorrectly. It should be spelled **great**. Like the title, each sentence contains one word that is spelled incorrectly. Correct the mistake in each sentence by crossing out the incorrect word and writing the correct word in the space after the number.

1. _____ We had a grate time at our family party.

2. _____ Grandfather told an interesting tail about his younger days.

3. _____ He related to us how his family had to whether the storm during the Depression.

4. _____ Their were many sacrifices to be made.

5. _____ His neighbors were find three dollars for breaking the law.

6. _____ The family didn't have the money and tried to take out a lone.

7. _____ Grandfather's parents offered to pay the hole fine for them.

8. _____ Our social studies class had red about the Depression last year.

9. _____ The eighth grade students discussed how sum of the people were begging in the streets during this time.

10. _____ Nun of us want to see another Depression.

11. _____ Obviously, the suns and daughters of the poor families experienced many problems.

12. _____ Our class president, Kristy Murray, maled away for information on the immigrants who came to America during the Depression.

13. _____ More peaces of information about these people will help us to have more appreciation for these unfortunate people.

14. _____ Some very wealthy families still had enough money to hire mades and butlers.

15. _____ The Depression will forever be remembered as a bleak period in America's passed.

89. DUE DO DEW YOU YEW KNOW NO SOME SUM HOMOPHONES?

Before you think your eyes are playing tricks on you, don't despair! The title shows examples of homophones, words that sound the same but are spelled differently and have different meanings. Sixteen homophonic words and their definitions appear below. Match the correct definition with its homophone. Then write your answers in the Magic Square. If your answers are correct, all columns and rows will add up to the same number. When you are finished, write the homophone for each of the sixteen words. Have fun!

A. BRED   E. CHEWS   I. HIRE   M. FLOWER
B. CHILI   F. WREST   J. GROAN   N. CYMBAL
C. MINOR   G. HEIR   K. DOUGH   O. AURAL
D. BIER   H. INTENTS   L. LEASED   P. WASTE

1. cultivated
2. instrument
3. moan
4. bites
5. successor
6. rented
7. garbage
8. juvenile

9. by ear
10. coffin
11. aims
12. bread mixture
13. employ
14. take from
15. hot pepper
16. plant

A	B	C	D
E	F	G	H
I	J	K	L
M	N	O	P

90. TWO-WORD DEFINITIONS FOR THOSE CONFUSING HOMOPHONES

This activity will help you remember the meanings of certain homophones. The nouns that are homophones are in Column A and the verbs that are homophones are in Column B. Circle the word that is defined in each question.

Column A	Column B
1. the animal (bare, bear)	1. to conquer (beat, beet)
2. the tree (beach, beech)	2. to vend (cell, sell)
3. the vegetable (beat, beet)	3. to expire (die, dye)
4. the drink (beer, bier)	4. to leave (flea, flee)
5. the color (blew, blue)	5. to ice (freeze, frieze)
6. the crack (brake, break)	6. to moan (groan, grown)
7. the basement (cellar, seller)	7. to greet (hail, hale)
8. the singers (choir, quire)	8. to mend (heal, heel)
9. the officer (colonel, kernel)	9. to require (knead, need)
10. the advice (council, counsel)	10. to tie (knot, not)
11. the cost (fair, fare)	11. to send (mail, male)
12. the insect (flea, flee)	12. to hurt (pain, pane)
13. the illness (flew, flu, flue)	13. to rest (pause, paws)
14. the plant (flour, flower)	14. to hunt (pray, prey)
15. the couple (pair, pare, pear)	15. to lift (raise, raze)
16. the aircraft (plain, plane)	16. to kill (slay, sleigh)
17. the rule (principal, principle)	17. to ogle (stair, stare)
18. the odor (reek, wreak)	18. to loot (steal, steel)
19. the story (tail, tale)	19. to swim (wade, weighed)
20. the number (to, too, two)	20. to don (ware, wear)

91. DOUBLE SIXES

If you identify the eight sentences that have underlined words used incorrectly, the total of the sentences will be 66. Thus, since the first sentence uses a word incorrectly, that is one. Circle the numbers of the other seven sentences whose underlined words are used incorrectly and then total them up. For each incorrectly used word, write the correct word in the space after the sentence. The first one is done for you.

1. He was <u>already</u> for the important game. ____all ready____

2. The rocket began its <u>ascent</u> into space. _____

3. The musical director was happy with the <u>number</u> of students attending the concert. _____

4. <u>Bring</u> the book to the library with you today. _____

5. I have never received such a wonderful <u>compliment</u> about my eyes. _____

6. We will certainly have to <u>chose</u> the best method before we start. _____

7. Would you like the strawberry shortcake for <u>dessert</u>? _____

8. Massachusetts is <u>further</u> north than Delaware. _____

9. Doctor, do you think this will <u>heel</u> in time for Saturday's game? _____

10. Please <u>let</u> me do this problem at my desk. _____

11. Iron is a widely used <u>meddle</u>. _____

12. When we were not paying attention, the celebrity walked right <u>passed</u> us. _____

13. Coffee is the <u>principal</u> export of Brazil. _____

14. The police erected barricades around the <u>scene</u> of the crime. _____

15. Warren wondered where the Roe family members parked <u>there</u> cars. _____

The eight sentences are: _____, _____, _____, _____, _____, _____, _____, and _____.

92. HAVE YOU EVER HAD DESSERT IN THE DESERT?

Does this sound like a silly question? If you know the difference in the two words' meanings and spellings, the question makes sense, in a silly way at least. This activity features thirty-five words that can be troublesome. Fill in the crossword.

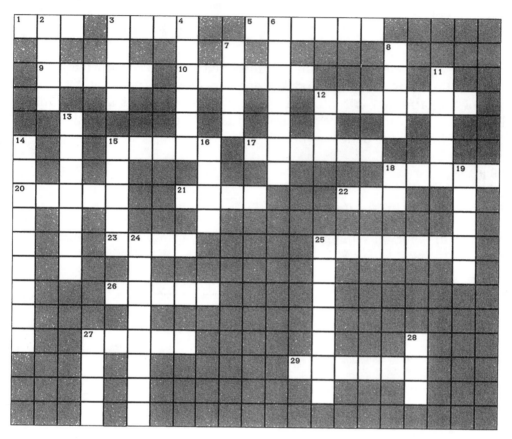

ACROSS	DOWN
1. to stop living	2. a small island
3. lower part of something	3. a fish
5. to receive	4. preposition meaning other than
9. not tight	6. advice
10. a representative of a country	7. past tense of know
12. food served after the main meal	8. to misplace
15. space or compartment	11. device used to stop a vehicle
17. dry, sandy region	12. to change the color of something
18. to separate or crack	13. group which advises
20. a person who is not yet an adult	14. to come to a new country
21. to send through the post office	15. process of being born
22. to purchase	16. to restore to health
23. the back part of the foot	18. preposition meaning near
25. city or money	19. space between two rows
26. one who works in the mines	24. to go out of the country to live in another
27. what is right or wrong	25. a building
29. spirit or mental condition	27. opposite of female
	28. original; opposite of old

Name _____ Date _____ Period _____

93. WORDS WE OFTEN CONFUSE

Do you know the difference between the words **threw** and **through**? Do you know when to use **sight** and not **cite** or **site**? This activity will test your mettle! Fill in the appropriate letters as you deal with words we often confuse.

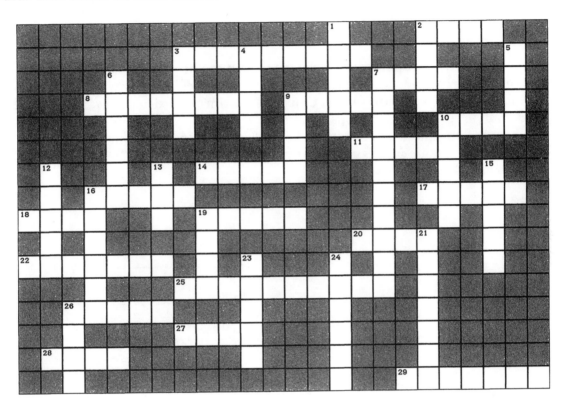

ACROSS

2. the opposite of pleasure
3. workers
7. spiritual part of a human being
8. private
9. opposite of wrong
10. a portion of a window
11. to rob
14. an aircraft
16. an award or prize
17. the act of seeing
18. to quote
19. not loud
20. to stay in a place in anticipation of something
22. the atmosphere's condition
25. referring to paper and envelopes
26. an element
27. a location
28. food from an animal
29. a conjunction displaying a choice

DOWN

1. to assess the worth or weight of something
2. to flow freely
3. not wealthy
4. single
5. a small opening in the skin
6. to interfere
7. not permanent
9. a ceremony
10. not complicated or fancy
12. to inscribe
13. a route
15. past tense of to throw
16. nerve or courage
19. to stop; to cease; to leave a job
21. preposition meaning in one side and out of the other
23. a hard metal
24. unit of heaviness
26. to encounter

94. TAKING A COMPUTER APART

Before you go to get the screwdrivers, please listen. You are not being asked to disassemble an expensive computer. Instead, this is a timed contest. Construct as many words as you can from the letters found in the word **computer**. Can you find thirty words or more? Each word must be at least four letters long. No proper names are allowed. Since there are eight different letters in the word **computer**, no letter can be used more than once. Your teacher will tell you how long you will have to do this word game. Write your words in the spaces below these directions. Good luck!

1. _____   16. _____

2. _____   17. _____

3. _____   18. _____

4. _____   19. _____

5. _____   20. _____

6. _____   21. _____

7. _____   22. _____

8. _____   23. _____

9. _____   24. _____

10. _____   25. _____

11. _____   26. _____

12. _____   27. _____

13. _____   28. _____

14. _____   29. _____

15. _____   30. _____

95. WHERE HAVE ALL THE LETTERS GONE?

Each of these thirty words has a letter missing. On the line next to each word spell the misspelled word correctly. Then on the line below the last question, write the letters, in order, that you added to spell these words correctly. These letters will spell out four famous names.

1. disatisfied _____
2. occasionlly _____
3. morgage _____
4. cortesy _____
5. arival _____
6. anihilate _____
7. aparatus _____
8. blaspemy _____
9. mischef _____
10. awfuly _____
11. miniture _____
12. adendum _____
13. changable _____
14. penicilin _____
15. aproval _____

16. ryme _____
17. frend _____
18. towrd _____
19. gramar _____
20. sophmore _____
21. stubborness _____
22. writen _____
23. aeril _____
24. conive _____
25. temperture _____
26. imature _____
27. anlysis _____
28. releve _____
29. unecessary _____
30. succed _____

Write each word's new letter on this line to spell out four famous names. _____,
_____, _____, and _____

96. HEADLINE READS "DID THE BELL OF THE BAWL DIE HER HARE?"

Wow! The local newspaper could use somebody to proofread its material. This headline with several misspellings is certainly embarrassing. Please help by finding 45 misspellings in the following paragraphs. Circle each misspelled word and spell it correctly on the back of this page. Each numbered line, 1-14, may have more than one misspelled word.

1. Marie always wanted to rite her life's story. She did knot no if she was going to

2. tell awl of it, but weather she told the hole story or not, it wood bee very interesting. Her

3. deer mother and father had razed her to be grate. Marie had herd there words and

4. followed they're advice. Each weak Marie set her hart on reaching important goals.

5. Sum of these included being rich enough two have a made and chef who would

6. cook stake four her. Marie's pried allowed for nothing less. She did not think of

7. herself as vane. After all, she wasn't like a raining queen on a thrown!

8. Though it was a soar point to bring up in conversation, stile was a principle

9. concern but not a vise for Marie. She imagined herself walking down the church's

10. isle with flours in her hands. The quire's singing would be herd bye each guessed.

11. It would be a tail Marie could tell her sun about in do thyme, years after his

12. berth.

13. Whatever becomes of pour Marie, wee sea that her plans will be hard to meat

14. and beet!

97. LUCKY SEVEN...LUCKY THIRTEEN SPELLING

Both sections of spelling words have seven groups. Each group has one misspelled word. Circle the misspelled word and then spell it correctly on the line following that group's last word. Then add up the numbers given to each misspelled word and you should come up with a total of 13 for that section. Thus, since **colossal** is misspelled in the first group, you have one point as you work your way to 13. Each section's total equals 13.

SECTION ONE

Group One : (1) colossle (2) changeable (3) liquor (4) reveal _____

Group Two: (1) occurence (2) rehearsal (3) resources (4) obeyed _____

Group Three: (1) feminine (2) cemetery (3) potent (4) grasious _____

Group Four: (1) weaken (2) agreement (3) reactien (4) fragrant _____

Group Five: (1) attention (2) utterence (3) resound (4) choices _____

Group Six: (1) twelvth (2) temperament (3) supersede (4) impish _____

Group Seven: (1) sieze (2) tendency (3) efficient (4) parody _____

SECTION TWO

Group One: (1) enlarge (2) example (3) agille (4) encourage _____

Group Two: (1) heredity (2) deciet (3) dissatisfied (4) ninety _____

Group Three: (1) endeavor (2) proof (3) symbolic (4) stuborn _____

Group Four: (1) consistant (2) prophesy (3) suppress (4) imply _____

Group Five: (1) buriel (2) malicious (3) safety (4) necessary _____

Group Six: (1) dilema (2) sponsor (3) unequal (4) friendly _____

Group Seven: (1) nutritian (2) prevalent (3) statistics (4) picnicking _____

98. MAKING THE SPELLING CONNECTION

Match the first part of the word with its second part. You might want to time yourself to see how quickly you can match the parts of these twenty words. Write the correct letter from Column B in the appropriate space next to each number in Column A.

Column A	Column B
1. _____ segre	A. ence
2. _____ adoles	B. ender
3. _____ hypo	C. versial
4. _____ diag	D. more
5. _____ lieut	E. enant
6. _____ resist	F. tery
7. _____ turbul	G. nique
8. _____ surr	H. nosis
9. _____ homo	I. logue
10. _____ reser	J. alent
11. _____ succ	K. ance
12. _____ tech	L. tion
13. _____ promo	M. geneous
14. _____ contro	N. cent
15. _____ sopho	O. voir
16. _____ epi	P. morphosis
17. _____ ceme	Q. ession
18. _____ bene	R. crite
19. _____ prev	S. gate
20. _____ meta	T. ficial

99. SPELLING EASE

In order to do well with this activity, it would be helpful to pay attention to the activity's title and to know what a pun is. One word in each group of three words is misspelled. Circle the word and spell it correctly in the space next to the question number. If you have identified each misspelled word and then spelled it correctly, you will understand this paragraph's first sentence. Good luck!

1.	_____	absince	fortunate	wearisome
2.	_____	regular	mischeif	fragrance
3.	_____	effective	homonym	presidant
4.	_____	accidint	throughout	confusion
5.	_____	government	speciman	vicinity
6.	_____	license	hospital	medecine
7.	_____	villain	omitted	souvinir
8.	_____	benefit	arguement	genius
9.	_____	advertise	inforcement	governor
10.	_____	fictitious	censor	exaggarate
11.	_____	specific	graduate	flagrent
12.	_____	forfit	grateful	excellent
13.	_____	lightning	atheletics	sophomore
14.	_____	genaral	latitude	grievous
15.	_____	privelege	reasonable	beverage
16.	_____	business	corraspond	recognize
17.	_____	literature	sulfer	manual
18.	_____	critical	critique	treaserer
19.	_____	principel	racket	solemn
20.	_____	maudlin	illitirate	elegant

100. AN EVEN HUNDRED

Eight of the words below are misspelled. Spell the word correctly in the space provided after the word. Add up the numbers of these words and the total is 100! For the other twelve correctly spelled words, leave the space blank.

1. offend _____

2. privilege _____

3. leisure _____

4. seperate _____

5. difficult _____

6. criticle _____

7. knowledge _____

8. discipline _____

9. valuable _____

10. diameter _____

11. colum _____

12. burgler _____

13. prefered _____

14. hydrogen _____

15. orchestra _____

16. sucess _____

17. distinguished _____

18. ignerance _____

19. vacuum _____

20. beleive _____

The words that are spelled incorrectly are _____, _____, _____,

_____, _____, _____, _____, and _____.

101. IS IT I BEFORE E OR E BEFORE I?

Words with the **ei** or **ie** combination often confuse even the best spellers. Ten of these words below use the **ei** combination and ten use the **ie** combination. If you have filled in the missing letters correctly, the ten words using the **ei** combination add up to 105. The words using the **ie** combination will do the same.

1. bel ____ f

2. br ____ f

3. spec ____ s

4. anc ____ nt

5. ach ____ ve

6. h ____ ght

7. sl ____ gh

8. rec ____ pt

9. th ____ r

10. v ____ l

11. dec ____ t

12. for ____ gn

13. l ____ sure

14. r ____ ns

15. n ____ ther

16. rel ____ ve

17. front ____ r

18. pr ____ st

19. f ____ ld

20. consc ____ nce

102. NICKELS AND DIMES, DOLLARS AND CENTS

The thirty letters that make up the six words above are taken from the thirty words below. Each of the thirty words has one of the above letters missing from it. On the line next to each number, write the letter that is missing from the word and indicate where it belongs by drawing an asterisk above the proper space. The first one is done for you. Cross off the letters in the title to keep track of the letters you have used as you move along in the exercise.

1. __K__ picnicing

2. _____ Wenesday

3. _____ obsene

4. _____ recomend

5. _____ paralel

6. _____ colum

7. _____ adition

8. _____ anoy

9. _____ adiction

10. _____ Hawai

11. _____ incidentaly

12. _____ acustom

13. _____ succed

14. _____ atendance

15. _____ extraorinary

16. _____ boundry

17. _____ anounce

18. _____ sethe

19. _____ interupt

20. _____ practicaly

21. _____ necesary

22. _____ approch

23. _____ temperment

24. _____ suppres

25. _____ occason

26. _____ leisur

27. _____ unecessary

28. _____ excesive

29. _____ concious

30. _____ miscellaneus

103. FILLING IN THE MISSING LETTERS

The letter that has been left out of each word appears to the left of the word. Draw an asterisk (*) above the space where the letter should appear. Then, in the parentheses following the word, write the number position of the letter you inserted. Thus, in number one of Group 1, **i** is the fifth letter of the word **gracious**, so you would write the number 5 in the parentheses. Add up the numbers in each group and the totals should be Group 1...22, Group 2...25, Group 3...23, and Group 4...18. Good luck!

Group 1

1. i...grac*ous (5)

2. i...pecular (   )

3. c...consious (   )

4. h...rhytm (   )

5. p...sychology (   )

Total points   (22)

Group 2

1. c...disipline (   )

2. i...circut (   )

3. a...sergent (   )

4. b...doutful (   )

5. m...remeber (   )

Total points   (25)

Group 3

1. d...Wenesday (   )

2. i...medeval (   )

3. r...Febuary (   )

4. b...probaly (   )

5. a...vengence (   )

Total points   (23)

Group 4

1. i...seze (   )

2. c...artic (   )

3. h...sympony (   )

4. e...manuver (   )

5. b...sutle (   )

Total points   (18)

104. FORMING PLURALS

To form the plural of ten of these nouns, spelling changes are necessary. For the other ten nouns, the singular and plural forms are spelled exactly the same way. If your answers are correct, the total of the numbers whose spellings remain the same is <u>100</u>.

Singular	Plural
1. belief	_____
2. surf	_____
3. Swiss	_____
4. elf	_____
5. scissors	_____
6. foot	_____
7. die	_____
8. child	_____
9. moose	_____
10. politics	_____
11. mouse	_____
12. sheep	_____
13. series	_____
14. salmon	_____
15. deer	_____
16. ox	_____
17. corps	_____
18. woman	_____
19. thief	_____
20. tornado	_____

© 1998 by John Wiley & Sons, Inc

105. COURTING PLURALS

If you select the correct plural form of the fifteen words in parentheses, you will spell out, in consecutive letters, a British word and its American equivalent. Then the activity's title becomes clearer. In the space provided, write the letter of the correct plural form and then write the letters in the spaces after the last question.

_____ 1. (donkey)   a. donkies   b. donkeys   c. donkeyes

_____ 2. (tomato)   a. tomatoes   b. tomatos   c. tomattos

_____ 3. (criterion)   q. criterions   r. criteria   s. criterio

_____ 4. (moose)   r. moose   s. meese   t. mooses

_____ 5. (goose)   h. gooses   i. geese   j. geeses

_____ 6. (ox)   s. oxen   t. oxes   u. oxus

_____ 7. (faculty)   r. facultys   s. faculti   t. faculties

_____ 8. (loaf)   d. loafs   e. loaves   f. loafs

_____ 9. (x)   r. x's   s. xes   t. xs

_____ 10. (brother-in-law)   l. brothers-in-law   m. brother-in-laws   n. brothers-in-laws

_____ 11. (studio)   a. studios   b. studioes   c. studi

_____ 12. (crisis)   w. crises   x. crisi   y. crisses

_____ 13. (wife)   x. wifes   y. wives   z. wiffes

_____ 14. (child)   d. childs   e. children   f. childrens

_____ 15. (tankful)   p. tankfull   q. tankfulls   r. tankfuls

The British word is _____ and its American equivalent is _____.

106. ELIMINATING THE CONFUSION ABOUT POSSESSIVES AND APOSTROPHES

Those darn apostrophes! They keep on showing up in all sorts of places! When to put them in and when to leave them out is a problem. Here is an example. If two women own a building, is it the *women's building* or the *womens' building*? If you said *women's building*, you have inserted the apostrophe in the correct place. Let's put the whole issue of when we should and when we shouldn't use the apostrophe to rest. Identify each of the forty words below by writing the letter associated with its definition. Each letter is used at least once.

a. singular possessive noun
b. plural possessive noun
c. singular possessive pronoun
d. plural possessive pronoun

e. singular verb
f. incorrect usage
g. singular noun
h. plural noun

1. _____ goe's
2. _____ his
3. _____ goose's
4. _____ man's
5. _____ men's
6. _____ donkeys'
7. _____ Canada's
8. _____ follows
9. _____ its
10. _____ Hank's
11. _____ capital's
12. _____ girls'
13. _____ brothers-in-law
14. _____ hers
15. _____ mother-in-law's
16. _____ Chris's
17. _____ duchess'
18. _____ duchesses
19. _____ theirs
20. _____ one hour's

21. _____ strategy
22. _____ Nevada's
23. _____ sisters
24. _____ sister's
25. _____ sisters'
26. _____ fellow's
27. _____ sends
28. _____ winners'
29. _____ ours
30. _____ nobody's
31. _____ everybody's
32. _____ Gregory's
33. _____ female's
34. _____ her's
35. _____ somebodys
36. _____ ourselfs
37. _____ mine
38. _____ miners'
39. _____ people
40. _____ school's

107. LOOK WHAT'S MISSING!

Two question marks, twelve commas, two colons, four hyphens, two sets of quotation marks, thirteen periods, and two semi-colons are missing from these sentences. Insert these punctuation marks in the correct positions within the sentences.

1. I have found the answer

2. Can you remember her telephone number

3. In the middle of the movie we heard a scream

4. Your coach the man in the brown coat is friendly

5. Though my friend is loud he is not obnoxious

6. I distinctly heard him say You're the one we have chosen

7. John was given a specialized CD player it was his first one

8. He arrived at 8 47 and left and 10 32

9. Dottie is a hard working intelligent woman

10. There are thirty two pencils in the box

11. Gary aren't you going to the shop today

12. Bob would like to attend the sports conference today however he has to go to work at the mall

13. Ben has just won a ten speed bike

14. The score 71 21 shows how strong the Stamford basketball team really is

15. Wayne said I'll see you later and walked away

108. FORMING A SENTENCE WITH CAPITAL LETTERS

If you correctly capitalize those words that need capital letters, you will spell out a sentence with a message for today. Circle the first letters of the words requiring capitals and write these letters from these two brief stories, in consecutive order, to form the sentence with a message for you.

charles anthony reynolds owns several restaurants. princess eileen, located in dubuque, iowa, is one of his fancy restaurants. each of these establishments has been written up in meyer's, a worldwide publication. in south america and north america, people have been giving these restaurants rave reviews. norman childress, a renowned indiana critic, recommends the lamb and chocolate pudding. elegant surroundings provide a wonderful dining atmosphere. normally thursday night dinners are less expensive.

last august we drove cross country and saw some amazing sights. the highways and rivers were especially impressive. in the north we visited the homes of philanthropists theodore and edwina rawlings. mr. frank olsen served as our guide for these visits. residents in these towns were very friendly. shortly after that, we saw displays featuring the english and the indians. zoos in the western part of our country were fun and educational. everybody had a great time. the heat was not a problem. herbert ellison and dave andrews planned the trip. yes, we certainly had a great time!

The letters spell out the following sentence: _____

_____

_____.

109. BRITISH OR AMERICAN?

The twenty words below are having a contest to see which team, the British or the American, can score more points. Some of the spellings are British and some are American. In the space next to each number, write the letter B for British or A for American. The point value for each question is in parentheses after the word. Total up the points and see who wins the battle of the words — the British or the Americans!

1. _____ program (2)

2. _____ kilogramme (3)

3. _____ neighbour (1)

4. _____ theater (2)

5. _____ defence (2)

6. _____ centre (3)

7. _____ honor (1)

8. _____ pygmy (1)

9. _____ traveler (2)

10. _____ check (3)

11. _____ reflexion (1)

12. _____ medieval (2)

13. _____ fuze (2)

14. _____ cheque (3)

15. _____ advertize (3)

16. _____ gray (1)

17. _____ storey (2)

18. _____ wagon (2)

19. _____ draft (2)

20. _____ jail (1)

The total number of points earned by the British is _____.

The total number of points earned by the Americans is _____.

The _____ are the winners!

110. THE PUNCTUATION PLACE

Match these thirteen marks of punctuation with their uses. Each is used only once. Write the corresponding letter in the correct space. The first one is done for you. Then write the third letter of each correct answer (in order) on the line below the last question. These thirteen letters will spell out three words.

a. apostrophe [']   f. ellipsis [...]   j. period [.]

b. brackets [[ ]]   g. exclamation mark [!]   k. question mark [?]

c. colon [:]   h. hyphen [–]   l. quotation marks [" "]

d. comma [,]   i. parentheses [( )]   m. semicolon [;]

e. dash [—]

1. __e__ to show an abrupt change of thought

2. _____ between independent clauses not joined by a coordinating conjunction

3. _____ to enclose explanations not part of a quotation

4. _____ to show that material has been omitted from a sentence

5. _____ between the hour and the minute when in writing

6. _____ to divide a word at the end of a line

7. _____ to enclose incidental explanatory material not considered important

8. _____ to enclose titles of short stories, poems, and essays

9. _____ to separate items in a series

10. _____ after a forceful interjection

11. _____ to form the possessive case of a singular noun

12. _____ after an abbreviation

13. _____ after a question

Each answer's third letter should be written in order on this line. Three words are formed.

s_____, _____, _____

© 1998 by John Wiley & Sons, Inc

111. CHECKING ON THE 75% EFFECTIVE SENTENCE CHECKER

Experience has taught us that the infamous 75% effective sentence checker needs someone to check on him! He seems to get three-quarters or 75% of his work correct; the other one-quarter, or 25%, is where you come in. Since three of the four underlined sections of each sentence are correct (there's the 75%), you must correct the one underlined section that is incorrect (that's the 25%). The errors could be in spelling, grammar, usage or mechanics. Circle the incorrect section and write the corrected version on the space following the sentence. Then the 75% effective sentence checker will be, with your able assistance, 100% correct!

1. Since we <u>gone</u> to see the movie on <u>Tuesday</u>, we have not stopped talking <u>about</u> <u>it</u>.
   _____

2. <u>Though</u> the movie was very <u>frightening</u> and <u>unforgettable</u>, Paula did not feel that she was <u>effected</u> by the graphic scenes. _____

3. A group of young <u>boys'</u> sat <u>beside</u> me and talked <u>softly</u> <u>throughout</u> the film. _____

4. <u>Although</u> <u>them</u> talking disturbed us, we could still enjoy the thrilling chase <u>scenes</u> involving about <u>twenty-five</u> motorcycles. _____

5. Those who <u>saw</u> the film <u>had</u> several questions <u>concerning</u> the <u>amount</u> of violent scenes in the last part of the film. _____

6. When David spoke with Dan and <u>I</u> about the film, we <u>could</u> not decide why the <u>protagonist</u> reacted so violently to the <u>mayor's</u> decision. _____

7. Unfortunately for the people in the village, the outlaw was <u>quite</u> vicious and <u>neither</u> the mayor <u>nor</u> the members of his police force <u>was</u> able to control this mean character.
   _____

8. <u>It</u> was <u>me</u> who thought that this <u>vengeful</u> character represented the evil aspects found in <u>today's</u> society. _____

9. <u>Weather</u> I am correct in my opinion <u>remains</u> to be seen, <u>but</u> I feel confident enough to argue my point with <u>others</u>. _____

10. <u>Needless to say</u>, this movie <u>does</u> stir up <u>controversey</u> and is not an easy movie to <u>understand</u>. _____

Section Five

COMPOSITION & PUBLIC SPEAKING

112. GETTING THE SENTENCE STRAIGHT

Each of these sentences has been scrambled. Unscramble each and write the words in the correct order on the line below. The number in parentheses after the sentence indicates the position of the underlined word in the unscrambled version of the sentence.

1. the left beret was the door near black. (7)

_____

2. program television was the interesting? (4)

_____

3. wallet been your expensive must very have. (2)

_____

4. seldom Sunrise Mike to Highway located goes on supermarket the. (2)

_____

5. trophy Tom's and take I to Rita the house will. (7)

_____

6. of taller twins which is the? (2)

_____

7. funny you Ronnie realize is ever how did? (6)

_____

8. is game over this card! (4)

_____

9. be you lesson let for a this! (3)

_____

10. it bring here. (2)

_____

113. SENTENCE DIRECTIVES

Call this activity "directed creativity." Below each line is a part of speech. Insert a word that fulfills the required part of speech in each blank. The key for the abbreviations used is found below the last sentence. The first one is done for you.

1. <u>He</u>   <u>saw</u>   <u>the</u>   <u>movie</u>   <u>last</u>   <u>night</u>.
   pro.   v.   adj.   n.   adj.   n.

2. _____ _____ _____ _____
        prep.   adj.   n.   pro.

   _____ _____
        advb.   v.

3. _____ _____ _____ _____
        adj.   adj.   n.   v.

   _____ _____ _____ _____
        adj.   n.   prep.   adj.

   _____ _____ _____ _____
        adj.   n.   prep.   n.

4. _____ _____ _____ _____
        advb.   v.   adj.   n.

   _____ _____
        prep.   pro.

5. _____ _____ _____ _____
        adj.   n.   v.   advb.

   _____ _____ _____
        prep.   adj.   n.

n. = noun pro. = pronoun v. = verb adj. = adjective advb. = adverb prep. = preposition

114. COMBINING SENTENCES

In the spaces provided, combine the following groups of sentences into one sentence. You may add or delete words as long as the original ideas are still there. The first one is done for you.

1. John is an eighth-grader. He is the oldest in his family. John attends Lake Shore Junior High School. John's last name is Stevens.

   <u>John Stevens, an eighth-grader at Lake Shore Junior High School, is the oldest in his family.</u>

2. The exercise machine cost $1,200. The family used to keep it in the basement. They recently moved it into the den. Now they use the exercise machine more often.

   _____

   _____

3. We walked along the beach today. Today is Sunday. The sun was out. There were only a few people at the beach today.

   _____

   _____

4. His friend attends Colgate University. Bob is John's friend's name. Bob wants to be a doctor. He will go to medical school after he graduates from Colgate University.

   _____

   _____

5. This summer we will visit Cape Cod. It is located in Massachusetts. On Cape Cod, we will fish, bike, and swim. We have vacationed there for the past six summers.

   _____

   _____

6. Today I am going to have a test in social studies class. The test will cover the American Revolution. There will be twenty short answers and one essay question. Mr. Redmond is my social studies teacher.

   _____

   _____

7. Ten inches of snow fell today. My father used the snow blower to remove the snow from our driveway. It took him two hours to do the job.

   _____

   _____

8. The dance will be held this Friday night in the gym. The cost is five dollars per person. Tickets will be available at the door.

   _____

   _____

115. THE CORRECT ORDER OF THINGS

In each group below, the sentences from the original paragraph have been taken out of order. Write the letter that correctly shows the original order. Be prepared to support your answers.

1. (A) Look for the three holes in the ball. (B) Insert your fingers in the holes. (C) Finally, hold the ball near your shoulder and face the lane. (D) Lift the bowling ball from the rack.

2. (A) Still another type is the one who wonders what is going on. (B) Another type is the one who waits for things to happen. (C) There are three kinds of people in this world. (D) One type is the person who gets things done.

3. (A) He questions the sense of even asking such a question. (B) Poet Robert Frost raises this question in one of his poems. (C) Now do you think the world will end in fire or ice? (D) Will the earth end in fire or ice?

4. (A) I will never forget the day my grandfather was rushed to the hospital. (B) In the hospital the attending doctor said that grandpa had had a heart attack. (C) My father went with grandpa in the ambulance. (D) Luckily, everything worked out since my grandfather was released a week later.

5. (A) As usual, the parade ended after the Fire Department marched by. (B) Last Saturday our town held its Fourth of July parade. (C) Following directly behind our town's leader was the Mintany High School Marching Band. (D) The parade was led by Mrs. Nancy Tarantino, our mayor.

116. STRINGING SENTENCES TOGETHER

There are ten subjects, ten predicates, and ten completers found in the three columns below. In the space below these columns, form ten sentences by stringing a subject, verb, and a completer together. Each is used only once.

Subjects	Verbs	Completers
The expensive ring	broke	a city in Canada.
Galileo	covered	a commemorative Elvis stamp.
The living room couch	invented	at the department store.
The Olympic swimmer	is	by his enemies.
S.E. Hinton	issued	from Bentley's Jewelers.
Snow	was executed	much of the country.
A stray dog	was found	outside our school.
The traitor	was purchased	*The Outsiders*.
The U.S. Postal Service	was stolen	the pool record.
Vancouver	wrote	the telescope.

_____

_____

_____

_____

_____

_____

_____

_____

_____

_____

117. CAUSE AND EFFECT WITH SOME CLAUSES

This activity asks you to compose logical sentences by matching the fifteen causes with their effects. As an example, the two parts that form the answer for number one are: (1) <u>After you hand in your homework</u> and (o) <u>you should go to the principal's office</u>. In the space after the first part of the sentence, write the letter of the second part that logically completes the sentence. Each part is used only once.

1. After you hand in your homework, __o__

2. As soon as he hit his opponent, ____

3. As soon as I finish my homework, ____

4. If we want to become wealthy, ____

5. If you want to borrow the money, ____

6. Though he can't speak French fluently, ____

7. Though he is smart, ____

8. Unless it gets warmer, ____

9. Unless my coach changes his mind, ____

10. Unless the membership fee is reduced, ____

11. Until I improve my grades, ____

12. We refused to eat the food, ____

13. When you are old enough to drive, ____

14. Whenever I am nervous, ____

15. While Marcia was having her ears pierced, ____

a. because it was cold.

b. he does not do well in school.

c. he plans to visit Paris.

d. I bite my fingernails.

e. I can lend it to you.

f. I have to study on the weekends.

g. I'll buy you a car.

h. I will call you.

i. I won't be playing in tomorrow's game.

j. I won't go outside this house.

k. she was nervously tapping her feet on the floor.

l. the boxer covered his face.

m. we can expect our enrollment to decrease.

n. we must win the lottery.

o. you should go to the principal's office.

118. MOVING ALONG WITH TRANSITIONAL WORDS

Transitional words help you as a writer. They introduce and also join ideas. In the sentence, "Besides going to school, Mitch went to work yesterday," the word **besides** is a transitional word that joins the two ideas of going to school and going to work together. Circle the twenty-five transitional words including **besides** that are placed backwards, forward, diagonally, and up and down in this word search. Included words are listed below the puzzle.

```
H T Y L T G Z K W V V P O Y P X G A V F N W F V
F L L Z I N F D T P Y T W L F V F B L F Q Y Y W
T I G K C K Y X A S H W Q R L D X P H S C H D Z
H E N C E R E V O E R O M A T H E R E F O R E V
N V I A B N T W R D T Q E L R A O E W L N T D W
E B D F L F S W I I T S A I L F G V Z J S H R B
V Z R U Z L I K M S R Q N M Y T Q E Y G E U N H
E K O R W S Y Y X E E C W I N E H W B C Q S T L
R F C T E N Z P V B T R H S M R K O K S U N T Y
T T C H L M S Q N Z A P I Z Q W Q H T Q E D X H
H X A E R X J F P B L Y L T J A W U B C N C L N
E W W R T N V F L Q K N E V C R B K D Z T W Y J
L M M M D D C Z S D O T K H W D Y Q S G L V L Q
E Y F O Z B G L M O L S G J K R F Z V S Y T H K
S F R R Y H G B S H C F M L M P H T Z D C L L H
S S C E F J X D B K L X G D V K Z G W Y C V Y W
J X G Q F Z V R L K G R P V K S L G C Z W S T S
```

ACCORDINGLY	FURTHERMORE	MOREOVER	THEREFORE
AFTERWARD	HENCE	NEVERTHELESS	THUS
ALSO	HOWEVER	NEXT	WHEN
BESIDES	INSTEAD	OR	YET
BUT	LATER	OTHERWISE	
CONSEQUENTLY	LIKEWISE	SIMILARLY	
FINALLY	MEANWHILE	SOON	

119. TYING IDEAS TOGETHER

This activity will help you with brainstorming before you start to write your compositions and essays by giving you practice in tying words together with ideas. Each of the five sets has three words. What happens beyond that depends largely on where you take them. For each set find three common characteristics or functions that exist among all three words. Some may be stretched a little, but try to think of strong ways in which the words are connected. An example set is done for you. Write your answers in the spaces provided.

Example set: baseball...popcorn...wood

Common characteristics: (1) all are found at a major league baseball game; (2) all can be held in one hand; (3) all are manufactured

Set One: hair...nails...teeth

Common characteristics: _____

_____

_____

Set Two: book...hand...light

Common characteristics: _____

_____

_____

Set Three: bus...shoe...weather

Common characteristics: _____

_____

_____

Set Four: animals...mascara...travel

Common characteristics: _____

_____

_____

Set Five: glass...paper...school...

Common characteristics: _____

_____

_____

120. BRAINSTORMING...THE START OF THE WRITING PROCESS

Brainstorming, the flow of ideas, will help you to gather ideas for a writing assignment. By brainstorming, you allow your mind to expand and your ideas will come more easily.

Here are nine topics ready for your brainstorming. List your answers in the spaces provided. Relax and let the ideas come to you!

1. List three things that roll. _____, _____, _____

2. Who are three infamous people? _____, _____, _____

3. Name three machines that were not around a century ago. _____, _____, _____

4. What are three things that excite first graders? _____, _____, _____

5. What are three things that are old within a week? _____, _____, _____

6. Name three favorite vacation spots not in North America. _____, _____, _____

7. Name three of your current English teacher's favorite expressions. _____, _____, _____

8. Name three professional sports teams whose names are associated with flight. _____, _____, _____

9. What are three board games? _____, _____, _____

121. BRAINSTORMING INTO A COMPOSITION

Often the toughest part of an assignment is coming up with ideas for the writing. Brainstorming is an effective way to generate ideas for developing a topic. Sharing your ideas on a subject with others sometimes helps you to see other aspects of the topic.

Below are four topics that your group of four will consider. Each group member is responsible for recording the ideas the group generates for one of the four topics. Thus, if the topic were Transportation Problems, the group might come up with related ideas such as safety regulations, accidents (both human and mechanical), escalating costs of operating vehicles, fuel consumption, road conditions and maintenance, inclement weather situations, and more. If this generating of ideas is done correctly, each topic begins to be narrowed and then is more easily handled as you formulate the thesis for your composition.

In the space below record the ideas for one of the general topics in the group assigned to you by your teacher. Consider as many aspects of the topic as time allows.

Group One: Celebrities, Compact Discs, Television, Reading

Group Two: College, Your Town, Outdoor Sports, Working Out

Group Three: Teens, Pollution, Food, Smoking

Group Four: Parents, Fears, Animals, Phone Calls

Group Five: Radio, Stereotypes, The Next Century, Jobs

Group Six: Sports, Religions, Leaders, Law Enforcement

_____

_____

_____

_____

_____

_____

_____

_____

_____

_____

_____

_____

(Continue on the back of this page.)

122. NOW THAT'S A GREAT IDEA!

One of the first things we need to do as writers with a new assignment is brainstorm or think of ideas that we can write about in our composition or essay. This activity asks you to concentrate on brainstorming so that you can fine-tune your ideas. For each of the topics listed below, write three possible titles for compositions that focus on that topic. Be open-minded and creative at the same time. An example is done for you.

Example topic: Animals

Titles: (1) Protecting Animals (2) Caring for Animals   (3) The Rights of Animals

Rock Music (1) _____

(2) _____

(3) _____

Vacations (1) _____

(2) _____

(3) _____

Nutrition (1) _____

(2) _____

(3) _____

Computers (1) _____

(2) _____

(3) _____

Extracurricular Activities (1) _____

(2) _____

(3) _____

123. MAKING THE ESSAY EASY (PART ONE)

Anticipating the types of questions you will see on an essay test can greatly improve your grade. Will you be asked to review, relate, explain, define or compare? Knowing exactly what these and other possible instructions mean is critical to your doing well on the test.

Here are ten words often used in essay questions. Match the word in Column A with its correct definition in Column B by writing the letter in the space next to the number. If your answers are correct, the correct letters (in order) will spell out an object followed by its function. Then on the reverse side of this paper, write an example question for each word used in Column A. To simplify the process, use these two objects, a bicycle and an automobile. Discuss your answers with your classmates.

Column A	Column B
1. ____ compare	a. to show and stress the differences between two or more
2. ____ contrast	b. to point out the similarities (mostly) and the differences
3. ____ define	d. to set forth in words in a specific or definite way
4. ____ discuss	e. to make clear and intelligible
5. ____ explain	h. to establish the validity of; to give evidence or present facts
6. ____ justify	k. to consider and argue aspects of the issue
7. ____ prove	l. to survey, reexamine, or summarize
8. ____ relate	o. to show how two or more are connected or associated
9. ____ review	s. to offer a clear meaning
10. ____ state	t. to show why it is right or logically sound in thought and reason

124. MAKING THE ESSAY EASY (PART TWO)

Ten words used in essay questions are found in this matching column. Match the words in Column A with their definitions in Column B. If your answers are correct, your answer key letters will spell out what you will say after you learn these words. Write the letters from Column B next to the correct number in Column A.

Then write the letters (in order) underneath the last question to see what you will say.

Column A	Column B
1. ___ classify	(an) to determine the value or worth of using evidence
2. ___ describe	(Ao) to give specific examples, instances, or comparisons
3. ___ diagram	(ay) to follow the order of events or steps
4. ___ enumerate	(et) to specify or outline a list of facts
5. ___ evaluate	(il) to give a detailed account of in sequence or story form
6. ___ illustrate	(iw) to arrange in groups according to a system
7. ___ list	(lg) to sketch, or draw, or illustrate to explain
8. ___ outline	(nm) to number, or order, or sequence
9. ___ summarize	(ss) to concisely present the most important points
10. ___ trace	(ye) to organize the main and the less important points

What will you say now after you learn these words?

_____

If there is time, write a question for each word in Column A. Use **summer** and **winter** as the two ideas. Use your notebook or the reverse side of this paper.

125. SUPPORTING YOUR IDEAS

After you have chosen a topic, you must construct a topic sentence to support what you intend to prove in the composition or essay. Then this topic sentence, "Smoking is dangerous to one's health," must be proven using reasons or examples or facts. In your attempt to show the health threats involved with smoking, think of three ways you would try to prove that statement. By saying that smoking causes lung disease, yellows one's teeth, and decreases one's breathing ability, you are well on your way to proving that "Smoking is dangerous to one's health."

For each of the four topic sentences below, write three reasons supporting the opinion stated in the topic sentence. Use the lines below the topic sentence to write your reasons or examples.

Technology has made life less physically demanding.

Reason 1: _____

Reason 2: _____

Reason 3: _____

A teenager's life involves a good deal of stress.

Reason 1: _____

Reason 2: _____

Reason 3: _____

Having enough money to do the things one wants makes life much easier.

Reason 1: _____

Reason 2: _____

Reason 3: _____

Our school day should not be extended by another two hours.

Reason 1: _____

Reason 2: _____

Reason 3: _____

126. SOME FROM HERE AND SOME FROM THERE

Here's a challenge for you. Include the following ten requirements in a story of approximately 150 words. Keep the words as they are presented below. They may be inserted anywhere in the story. Underline the ten requirements so they are easily visible.

1. in the morning
2. foolishly
3. When the time had come,
4. rushing from the diner
5. until both people agreed

6. Needless to say,
7. friends
8. one at a time
9. computers
10. sandals and moccasins

_____
_____
_____
_____
_____
_____
_____
_____
_____
_____
_____
_____
_____
_____
_____
_____

(Continue on the back of this page.)

127. CREATING A SCENE

Dialogue, two or more characters talking to one another, is an important part of any story. In the space below create a dialogue for one of the following situations. Your characters' words should be realistic and interesting. Consult your text for the correct punctuation marks needed for your dialogue. Use the reverse side of this paper if more space is needed.

Situation A: Jerry, a seventeen-year-old male, is going to break up with sixteen-year-old, Laurie, his girlfriend of seven months. They are walking home after going to a movie. Begin the dialogue with Jerry saying, "Laurie, I've been thinking about you and me."

Situation B: Mr. Lawrence, the eighth-grade social studies teacher, has accused Frank, one of his students, of looking at another student's paper during today's exam. Unfortunately, Frank has cheated. Begin the dialogue with Mr. Lawrence saying, "Frank, I think you and I have to talk about something."

Situation C: You have been selected for the school athletic team or the dramatic production, but your best friend hasn't. Begin the dialogue with your friend saying, "I can't believe I wasn't selected."

_____

_____

_____

_____

_____

_____

_____

_____

_____

_____

_____

_____

_____

_____

_____

128. CREATING DIALOGUE

One of the writer's tasks is to construct dialogue that establishes mood. Starting with one of these first lines from an imaginary dialogue involving two characters you will invent, continue the dialogue as your characters' words exemplify the mood. Share your work with your classmates. Write away!

Choose one of these first lines.

1. "I never saw you act like this before!"   2. "How could you have told him that after you said you would tell nobody?"   3. "This is not what I asked for."   4. "You really didn't? Did you?"   5. "Should we let the others know about this?"

Choose one of these moods.

1. guilt   2. happiness 3. anger 4. surprise   5. sadness

Describe your two characters and name each.

Character's name _____

Description _____

_____

Character's name _____

Description _____

_____

Now write the dialogue here.

_____

_____

_____

_____

_____

_____

_____

_____

_____

_____

_____

© 1998 by John Wiley & Sons, Inc

(Continue on the back of this page.)

129. A DAY IN THE LIFE

Have you ever imagined being someone else for a day, a week, or longer? Most of us might want to be a supermodel, an outstanding professional athlete, a famous rock star, or someone else whose life seems to be fun and exciting. Here is your chance to live that life, at least on paper. In the space below recreate a typical day in the life of a person whose life you would like to live for a day. Use complete sentences, accurate verbs and adjectives, interesting images and events in this recreation.

A Day in the Life of _____

_____

_____

_____

_____

_____

_____

_____

_____

_____

_____

_____

_____

_____

_____

_____

_____

_____

_____

(Continue on the back of this page.)

130. SEEING IT FROM ANOTHER'S EYES

A writer has specific reasons for writing a book from the perspective of a certain character. Harper Lee chose Scout Finch, now an adult, to tell the story of the Maycomb, Alabama, community. How would the story have been different if it were told from her father's or her brother's perspective? Would "Casey at the Bat" have been much different had Casey, and not the narrator, told the story? If so, how?

Select a scene from a book, a poem, or another short work of fiction and retell the plot from another character's perspective. You can retell the plot in a serious manner, a humorous way, or a combination of the two. Choose a scene, brainstorm, and then have some fun telling the events from another's perspective.

I have selected to rewrite the plot (or scene) from the literary work
_____ by _____. I will retell it from the

perspective of the character named _____.

_____

_____

_____

_____

_____

_____

_____

_____

_____

_____

_____

_____

_____

_____

_____

(Continue on the back of this page.)

131. USING YOUR WRITER'S TOOLBOX

When composing a composition, an essay, or another piece of writing, you have many tools that you can readily use. Using sensory imagery, selecting the most appropriate diction, and constructing effective dialogue are some of the tools that help to create a positive effect upon your readers.

In this activity put some of these writer's tools to use as you compose a story, real or fictional, of about 200–250 words. After you have used each required tool listed below in your composition, place a check in the space next to the tool. In future writings continue to use these tools and even add more as your writing improves.

1. ___ Include at least two colors. 2. ____ Include an adverb ending with "-ing." 3. ___ Include the time and the place. 4. ___ Use at least three sensory images. 5. ___ Include three action verbs. 6. ___ Include five adjectives (besides the colors you have included). 7. ___ Use an opening line that grabs the reader's attention. 8. ___ Name any characters you include. 9. ___ Entitle your story. 10. ___ Vary the length and type of your sentences. 11. ___ End your story in an effective way.

_____

_____

_____

_____

_____

_____

_____

_____

_____

_____

_____

_____

(Continue on the back of this page.)

132. DESCRIBING A PERSON

Want to say something good about your friend? brother? sister? parents? Here are twelve positive adjectives used to describe a person. First choose a person you would like to describe. Then select ten adjectives. For each adjective write an example of how your selected person fits that adjective. Use one person for all ten descriptive words. An example is given for you.

Person: My friend Natalie

Descriptive word: reliable

Example: Natalie is always there for me when I need someone to talk to about a problem.

Adjectives:

alert	consistent	imaginative	perceptive
brilliant	gifted	interesting	sincere
cheerful	honest	methodical	thorough

My selected person is _____.

Descriptive word	**Example**
1._____	_____
2._____	_____
3._____	_____
4._____	_____
5._____	_____
6._____	_____
7._____	_____
8._____	_____
9._____	_____
10._____	_____

133. THE SPEECH'S PURPOSE

Knowing the purpose of your speech is critical since it gives direction to your words. Once the purpose is established, the other steps in writing a speech follow logically.

For each purpose below, write two topics that would befit the speech's purpose. The topics should be topics from your life. Be ready to explain your answers. One answer for the first topic is done for you.

Purpose	Appropriate topics
1. to inform	the dangers of smoking cigarettes
2. to persuade	
3. to introduce	
4. to move to action	
5. to accept	
6. to entertain	
7. to present	

134. A CHECKLIST FOR CONSTRUCTING AN EFFECTIVE SPEECH

Public speaking does not have to be a source of tension. There are many suggestions you can use for writing a memorable speech. Paying attention to the ideas listed below will help you become a more effective and convincing speaker.

Place a check next to any of the items you have used in constructing your speech. You do not have to include all of them in your speech's construction, but each will serve you well in your efforts. Be ready to explain why you have chosen to use the checked items.

1. The purpose of my speech is to (more than one is acceptable)

____ inform   ___ persuade

____ entertain   ___ other (specify) _____

2. In the beginning of my speech, I

___ tell a story or use an illustration   ___ ask a question

___ use a quotation   ___ establish a relationship with the audience

___ employ facts or statistics   ___ use humor

___ other (specify) _____

3. The body of my speech is organized mainly through

___ a cause and effect relationship   ___ chronological order

___ a comparison/contrast   ___ examples

___ an extended metaphor   ___ a problem and solution format

___ step-by-step logic   ___ other (specify) _____

4. I end my speech by using a(n)

___ anecdote   ___ appeal to the audience

___ convincing fact   ___ example or illustration

___ joke   ___ restatement of fact(s)

___ summary   ___ other (specify) _____

135. THE STYLE OF THE SPEECH

A speech has many important components. Its purpose, opening, main idea(s), and closing are crucial to its success. Yet, the speech's style or how your words are presented can really help to make your speech more effective and convincing.

While constructing and revising your speech, use these suggestions to make your speech the best it can be. All do not have to be used in one speech, but many should be included. For each item below, write an example of how you intend to use (or have used) the following techniques in your speech.

1. specific examples _____

2. personalize the speech _____

3. state (or infer) the purpose of the speech _____

4. clear transitions _____

5. restate an important point _____

6. clear thesis statement _____

7. variety of sentence length _____

8. vivid language _____

9. clear summary of your main points _____

10. convincing facts _____

11. inclusion of a rhetorical question _____

12. use an analogy _____

13. use parallel structure _____

14. conclude emphatically _____

15. include humor _____

136. THE PURPOSE BEHIND THE OPENING LINE

Ten interesting lines, either written or said by ten famous people, are written below. If each line were used as a speech's opening line, what would be the purpose the speaker is trying to accomplish by each line? Write your answer in the appropriate spaces.

1. "I have but one lamp by which my feet are guided, and that is the lamp of experience." Patrick Henry. _____

_____

2. "Yesterday is not ours to recover, but tomorrow is ours to win or lose." Lyndon B. Johnson. _____

_____

3. "Nobody can give you freedom." Malcolm X. _____

_____

4. "Love all, trust a few." William Shakespeare. _____

_____

5. "Music hath charms to soothe a savage breast/To soften rocks, or bend a knotted oak." William Congreve. _____

_____

6. "To be great is to be misunderstood." Ralph Waldo Emerson. _____

_____

7. "Do not consider painful what is good for you." Euripedes. _____

_____

8. "Character is much easier kept than recovered." Thomas Paine. _____

_____

9. "The persuasion of a friend is a strong thing." Homer. _____

_____

10. "What hunger is in relation to food, zest is in relation to life." Bertrand Russell.

_____

_____

137. LOOKING AT THE BEST

The speeches excerpted below are considered to be among the finest speeches in the English language. What makes them so noteworthy? In addition to an important message that is conveyed, each speech also uses effective opening lines, a well-crafted body, and a memorable conclusion.

The concluding lines of three great speeches are below. In the spaces provided, write why you think these lines are praiseworthy. Is it the message, appeal, diction, examples, or something else which contributes to its fame? Discuss your opinions with your classmates.

1. "...When we let freedom ring, when we let it ring from every tenement and every hamlet, from every state and every city, we will be able to speed up that day when all of God's children, black men and white men, Jews and Gentiles, Protestant and Catholics, will be able to join hands and sing in the words of the old spiritual, 'Free at last, free at last. Thank God Almighty, we are free at last.'" Martin Luther King's "I Have a Dream" speech delivered on August 28, 1963, in Washington, DC.

_____
_____
_____
_____

2. "...that we here highly resolve that these dead shall not have died in vain...that this nation, under God, shall have a new birth of freedom...and that government of the people...for the people...shall not perish from this earth." Abraham Lincoln's Gettysburg Address given on November 19, 1863, on the battlefield near Gettysburg, Pennsylvania.

_____
_____
_____
_____

3. "As I would not be a slave, so I would not be a master. This expresses my idea of democracy. Whatever differs from this, to the extent of the difference, is no democracy." Barbara Jordan, the first black woman to deliver a keynote address at the Democratic Party's national convention, quoting Abraham Lincoln on July 12, 1976.

_____
_____
_____
_____

138. PREPARING A SPEECH

You have been asked to deliver a speech about one of the following topics. Select one of the seven ideas below and explain what you would talk about if the speech had to be approximately four to seven minutes long. Write your ideas in the spaces provided for you. (Depending upon your teacher's request, this may serve as an outline or the finished copy.)

(a) Why movies are a popular form of entertainment (b) The need for a democracy (c) The world twenty years from today (d) Effective leadership is a necessity for success (e) Competition is more productive than destructive (f) The truth behind proverbs (g) Advertising's do's and don't's

_____

_____

_____

_____

_____

_____

_____

_____

_____

_____

_____

_____

_____

_____

_____

_____

_____

_____

_____

(Use the reverse side if necessary.)

139. CHOOSING AND SUPPORTING ONE OVER THE OTHER

For each pair of choices, select the one choice you favor more. Then write at least four reasons why you have made that choice. These supporting reasons must be substantial and logical. Whenever possible, use reason over emotion in making your selections. Write your answers in the spaces provided.

1. Which is the better season in your town — summer or winter?

_____

_____

_____

_____

2. Which sport is more physically demanding — soccer or basketball?

_____

_____

_____

_____

3. Where should more money be spent for research — AIDS or cancer?

_____

_____

_____

_____

4. Is it better to have health or wealth?

_____

_____

_____

_____

5. Who should be paid more — a surgeon or a popular movie star?

_____

_____

_____

_____

140. QUESTIONS ABOUT YOUR SPEECH

Below are ten vital concerns any speaker would have when preparing a speech. Certainly, the audience is an important concern. It is important to know who will be there. Are the audience members your age, older, or younger? Because of this, you might decide to word your speech differently. Will your examples be different because of who is sitting in front of you? Why?

In the spaces below each item, write two or more important considerations for each aspect of an effective speech.

1. What is the speech's purpose/objective?

_____

_____

2. What is the organizational pattern of your speech? Will you employ cause and effect, chronology, problem and solution, or another format? Why?

_____

_____

3. What kind of support will you use to make the speech convincing? Do you plan to use comparison and contrast, examples, facts, illustrations? Why?

_____

_____

4. What are some things about the audience you should know in preparing the speech?

_____

_____

5. How will you start the speech to attract the attention of your listeners?

_____

_____

6. What closing thoughts or strategies will you use?

_____

_____

7. Why will you choose (or not choose) to include visual or audio-visual aids in your speech?

_____

_____

8. From what materials have you gathered your information for the speech? How credible are these sources?

_____

_____

9. What strategies in your speech's construction have you included to make it is easier to memorize?

_____

_____

10. What have you learned in practicing your speech that will eventually make it better?

_____

_____

Section Six

LITERATURE

141. LITERARY TERMS CROSSWORD PUZZLE

Terms such as conflict, narrator, and setting are important terms used when discussing literature. In addition to these terms, twenty-two other literary terms are the answers to the clues for this crossword puzzle. Write the correct answers in the appropriate spaces within the puzzle.

ACROSS

3. conversation in a story or play
7. a unit of a novel
10. words creating mental pictures or images
11. part of the story in which the conflict is solved
15. person who writes a story
16. person who relates a story
18. book-length piece of fiction
21. figure of speech showing a comparison
22. an object used to represent something abstract
23. an interruption in the story showing an earlier scene

DOWN

1. struggle between characters
2. quality of being comical
3. a play
4. an account of a person's life written by that person
5. an invented story
6. speech recited by one character
7. person in a story
8. an account of a person's life written by another person
9. turning point of a work
12. time and place of a story
13. atmosphere or feeling in a work
14. literature about real persons or things
17. central idea or meaning of a story
19. a unit of a poem
20. the author's attitude toward the people, places, and events in his work

Name _____ **Date** _____ **Period** _____

142. LITERARY TERMS CONSTRUCTION SITE

Twenty-five literary terms are arranged in order by the number of letters found in each word. Insert the words in their correct spaces and then write the term's definition on a separate sheet of paper.

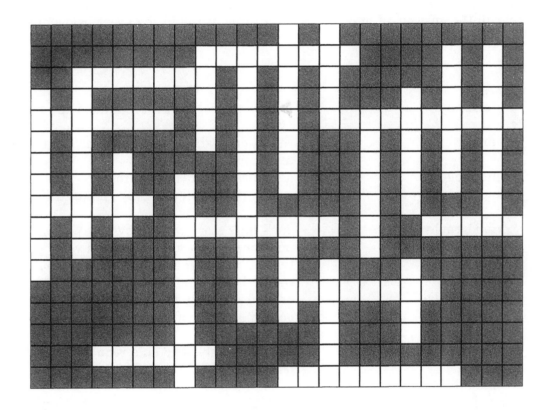

MOOD	CLIMAX	CHARACTER
TONE	IMAGERY	BIOGRAPHY
DRAMA	FICTION	FLASHBACK
NOVEL	CHAPTER	MONOLOGUE
THEME	SETTING	RESOLUTION
HUMOR	CONFLICT	NONFICTION
STANZA	NARRATOR	AUTOBIOGRAPHY
SYMBOL	DIALOGUE	
AUTHOR	METAPHOR	

143. SO MUCH TO READ, SO LITTLE TIME...

If you plan to travel across the country this summer, would you consult an atlas, anthology, or bibliography? An atlas is a book of maps so that is the book that could be useful to you. This activity asks you to distinguish between an almanac, a novel, and other forms of reading matter. Match the type of literature in Column A with its description in Column B. If the answers are correct, you will find the name of a famous race track, a man's name, and a synonym for tear in the answer column. Write those three words in the space below question number 20.

Column A	Column B
1. _____ almanac	a. literature dealing with real facts and real events
2. _____ annual	b. collection of short stories, poems, essays, and more
3. _____ anthology	c. a long work of fictional prose
4. _____ autobiography	d. a book published annually giving statistics on many subjects
5. _____ bibliography	e. one's life's story written by that person
6. _____ biography	f. publication that appears once a year
7. _____ commentary	g. type of literature based in the imagination of the author
8. _____ encyclopedia	h. ordinary form of written or spoken language
9. _____ essay	i. book consisting of examples or rules
10. _____ fiction	j. handbook
11. _____ gazetteer	k. magazine published on a regular basis
12. _____ journal	l. list of suggested readings
13. _____ manual	m. story of a person's life
14. _____ nonfiction	n. book giving information (published articles arranged alphabetically)
15. _____ novel	o. series of explanatory notes
16. _____ periodical	p. periodical devoted to business or industry
17. _____ prose	q. daily newspaper
18. _____ reference book	r. book used as a source of information that must be left in the library
19. _____ style book	s. dictionary of geographical names
20. _____ trade journal	t. article written to show the author's opinion on a topic

The famous race track is _____. The man's name is _____. The synonym for tear

is _____.

Name _____ Date _____ Period _____

144. NEWSPAPER AND MAGAZINE TERMS

Have some fun as you fill in the letters of this self-construct puzzle. Below the puzzle, thirty-one terms used in the newspaper and magazine fields are listed in order by the number of letters in each word. Once the puzzle is completed, you and your classmates can discuss these terms. One word has already been done for you.

ADVERTISING	EDITOR	READERSHIP
ANGLE	ENTERTAINMENT	REPORTER
AUDIENCE	FACTS	SCOOP
BUREAU	FREELANCE	SIDEBAR
BYLINE	HEADLINE	SLANT
CARTOONS	LIBEL	SOURCE
CIRCULATION	OBITUARY	STAFF
COLUMNIST	OPINION	STYLE
DATELINE	PHOTOGRAPHS	TABLOID
DEADLINE	QUERY	
EDITION	QUOTE	

145. RECOGNIZING LITERARY SYMBOLS

Literary symbols are used by authors to represent something else. A wedding ring could represent loyalty, a flag could represent patriotism, and an eagle could represent power. Thirty-two questions dealing with literary symbols are found in this crossword puzzle. Fill in the answers and remember these symbols as you encounter them in your future readings.

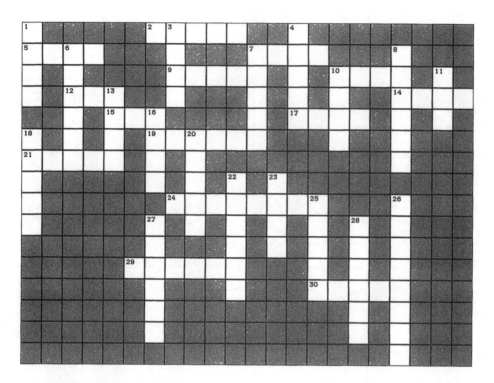

ACROSS

2. color symbolizing purity
5. direction symbolizing newness or birth
7. color symbolizing wealth
9. liquid symbolizing cleansing or birth
10. flower symbolizing beauty
12. color symbolizing blood or passion
14. animal symbolizing nobility
15. bird symbolizing wisdom
17. paternal authority figure
19. season symbolizing oncoming death
21. bird symbolizing might
24. god symbolizing strength
29. thing symbolizing transition
30. time symbolizing mystery or romance

DOWN

1. direction symbolizing death
3. bird symbolizing war
4. color symbolizing death
6. season symbolizing rebirth
7. color symbolizing envy or nature's freshness
8. color symbolizing cowardliness or brightness
10. thing symbolizing commitment
11. animal symbolizing slyness
13. bird symbolizing peace
16. animal symbolizing gentleness
18. goddess symbolizing beauty
20. animal symbolizing ferocity
22. things symbolizing justice
23. thing symbolizing patriotism
25. number symbolizing luck
26. number symbolizing that which is unlucky
27. color symbolizing royalty
28. action symbolizing freedom

146. WHAT DO YOU THINK THESE LITERARY QUOTATIONS MEAN?

In one of his poems, John Donne writes, "No man is an island..." What exactly does this mean to you? Obviously, Donne's words have special meaning since we have been quoting that line for nearly four centuries.

Here are ten famous lines from various literary works. In the space following each quotation, write what you think the author means by that line. Discuss your findings with your classmates.

1. "I wandered lonely as a cloud." (William Wordsworth, "Daffodils")

_____

_____

2. "Good fences make good neighbors." (Robert Frost, "Mending Wall")

_____

_____

3. "To thine own self be true." (William Shakespeare, *Hamlet*)

_____

_____

4. "A rose is a rose is a rose is a rose." (Gertrude Stein, "Sacred Emily")

_____

_____

5. "It was the best of times, it was the worst of times." (Charles Dickens, *A Tale of Two Cities*)

_____

_____

6. "I'm nobody! Who are you? Are you nobody, too?" (Emily Dickinson, an untitled poem)

_____

_____

7. "To be great is to be misunderstood." (Ralph Waldo Emerson, "Self Reliance")

_____

_____

8. " 'Tis better to have loved and lost than never to have loved at all." (Alfred, Lord Tennyson, "In Memoriam")

_____

_____

9. "A thing of beauty is a joy forever." (John Keats, "Endymion")

_____

_____

10. "...I have promises to keep, and miles to go before I sleep." (Robert Frost, "Stopping by Woods on a Snowy Evening")

_____

147. LET'S GET STARTED

How authors choose to start their stories is interesting. Sometimes the purpose is to describe a character or a setting or to introduce a situation. At other times, they create a mood from the very first word. In these eight first lines from various novels, explain what you feel each author's purpose is. Perhaps it is one of the purposes already mentioned or even a combination of them. It might also be some other purpose that is not one of these. Write your answers in the appropriate spaces. Be ready to explain your answers.

1. _____ When I saw the crowd gathering at the train station, I worried what President Roosevelt would think.
The Summer of My German Soldier by Bette Greene

2. _____ He was an old man who fished alone in a skiff in the Gulf Stream and he had gone eighty-four days now without taking a fish.
The Old Man and the Sea by Ernest Hemingway

3. _____ When I stepped out into the bright sunlight from the darkness of the movie house, I had only two things on my mind: Paul Newman and a ride home.
The Outsiders by S.E. Hinton

4. _____ I should of been in school that April day.
A Day No Pigs Would Die by Robert Newton Peck

5. _____ Now, I don't like school, which you might say is one of the factors that got us involved with this old guy we nicknamed the Pigman.
The Pigman by Paul Zindel

6. _____ They murdered him.
The Chocolate War by Robert Cormier

7. _____ I had the story, bit by bit, from various people, and, as generally happens in such cases, each time it was a different story.
Ethan Frome by Edith Wharton

8. _____ I went back to the Devon School not long ago, and found it looking oddly newer than when I was a student there fifteen years before.
A Separate Peace by John Knowles

On the reverse side of this paper write one opening line to (a) create mood, (b) introduce character, (c) describe a setting.

148. A SHAKESPEAREAN SONNET

One of the masters of the English language is William Shakespeare. In addition to his numerous plays, including *Romeo and Juliet, Hamlet, Julius Caesar,* and *Macbeth,* Shakespeare also wrote 154 sonnets, poems consisting of fourteen lines and written in a verse form called iambic pentameter. Iambic pentameter is a line of ten syllables having the odd-numbered syllables unaccented and the even-numbered syllables accented. The first line of this sonnet, "When in disgrace with Fortune and men's eyes," is an example of a line of iambic pentameter.

Read the following Shakespearean sonnet carefully and then on the lines provided answer the questions that follow.

Sonnet 29
When in disgrace with Fortune and men's eyes,
I alone beweep my outcast state,
And trouble deaf heaven with my bootless cries,
And look upon myself and curse my fate,
Wishing me like to one more rich in hope,   5
Featur'd like him, like him with friends possess'd,
Desiring this man's art, and that man's scope
With what I most enjoy contented least;
Yet in these thoughts myself almost despising,
Haply I think on thee; and then my state,   10
Like to the lark at break of day arising
From sullen earth, sings hymns at heaven's gate;
For thy sweet love rememb'red such wealth brings
That then I scorn to change my state with kings.

1. What is one word that depicts the speaker's mood or tone in the first four lines?

   _____

2. List four words or phrases found in those lines that support your answer for the previous question. _____

3. What is one word that depicts the mood or tone expressed by the speaker in lines 5–8?

   _____

4. List four words or phrases found in those lines that support your answer for the previous question. _____

5. What mood is expressed in lines 9–14? _____

6. List four words or phrases found in those lines that support your answer for the previous question. _____

7. What word in line 9 signifies a transition or change of mood? _____

8. What does the poet mean by his "state"? _____

9. Giving inanimate things human characteristics is called personification. What is an example of personification found in the third line of the sonnet? _____

10. Writing no more than four sentences, summarize the sonnet. _____

    _____

    _____

    _____

149. ANALYZING A POEM

Poet Dylan Thomas offered the following explanation of poetry. He said, "Poetry is what in a poem makes you laugh, cry, prickle, be silent, makes your toenails twinkle, makes you want to do this or that or nothing, makes you know that you are not alone in this unknown world, that your bliss and suffering is forever shared and forever all your own."

This activity offers some practical suggestions for appreciating poetry. Fill in the blanks and enjoy!

1. Name of poem _____

2. Poet _____

3. Who is the poem's speaker? _____

4. To whom, if anyone in particular, is the poem addressed? _____

    _____

5. What is the setting? _____

6. What is the poet's occasion for writing this poem? _____

    _____

7. What is the poem's main purpose? _____

    _____

8. What are some poetic devices used by the poet? List each and then tell why it is used.

    _____

    _____

    _____

    _____

9. What specific words (diction) help the poet convey the poem's message? Cite the line numbers. _____

    _____

    _____

10. Do you like the poem? Why? _____

    _____

    _____

150. SOMETHING (OR NOTHING) IN COMMON

Imagine that three literary characters from three different works you have read are brought together to share some good food and good conversation. What would they talk about? Would they agree on certain issues and disagree on others? Would one be more open-minded than the other two? Which would be the conservative one(s)?

Here are four questions that will be discussed during this imaginative meal. Based on the information you know about each character from your reading, write his or her answers to the following questions. Be ready to justify the character's response.

Please list your three characters in the appropriate spaces below this paragraph. Now the guests have arrived, the table is set, and the meal is ready to be served. Let the conversation begin!

Character 1 _____

Character 2 _____

Character 3 _____

Question 1: How important is friendship?

Character 1 _____

Character 2 _____

Character 3 _____

Question 2: When are you happiest?

Character 1 _____

Character 2 _____

Character 3 _____

Question 3: What is your opinion of the society in which you live?

Character 1 _____

Character 2 _____

Character 3 _____

Question 4: What type of people do you most admire?

Character 1 _____

Character 2 _____

Character 3 _____

151. EXTENDING THE LIFE OF THE LITERARY CHARACTER

Have you ever thought what Tom Sawyer or Huckleberry Finn would be like as adults? How would John and Lorraine from *The Pigman* or Scout Finch from *To Kill a Mockingbird* do in their adult years? What jobs would they have? Would they be happy? Would their views on life change or stay the same? Would they have children?

Select a character from a literary work that you have read. In the space below write a character sketch of this young character living as an adult in today's society. Some ideas you might want to include in the sketch are the character's looks, typical attire, occupation, ideas on certain issues (especially current controversial ones), family situation, what others say about the person, and other facts concerning the character. Upon completing the character sketch, share your ideas with your classmates.

_____

_____

_____

_____

_____

_____

_____

_____

_____

_____

_____

_____

_____

(Continue on the reverse side.)

152. JUDGING A CHARACTER

Coming to decisions about characters we meet in literary works is an interesting process. Why do we like or dislike a particular character? What goes into such a decision? Generally, we look at the character and then, to an extent, measure what we see against our own value systems.

This activity will help you to make sound judgments about literary characters. It will be useful for any character in any literary work. In the designated spaces fill in the information for the character you are studying. Have fun as you come to decisions concerning the merits of your character.

Character's name _____

Literary work in which he or she appears _____

Author _____

Type of literary work (novel, play, short story, poem) _____

1. What is the character's physical appearance? _____

_____

_____

2. What does the character do? _____

_____

_____

3. What does the character say? _____

_____

_____

4. What do others say about him or her? _____

_____

_____

5. What does the character think or feel? _____

_____

_____

6. What does the author say about the character? _____

_____

_____

153. NAMING YOUR CHARACTERS

The importance of appropriately naming characters in a literary work cannot be underestimated Often authors will search for the exact name that conveys a sense of who the character is. Goldilocks and The Big Bad Wolf are appropriate names to tell the reader something about these characters.

Here are ten descriptions of possible characters who, as of this moment, do not exist. Using the descriptions below, name each character, so that in hearing the name the reader has a sense of the character's traits. Be prepared to justify the names you've given to these characters.

1. a lonely, old man who is living in a poor neighborhood

   _____

2. a beautiful and wealthy California girl

   _____

3. the male owner of a local small-town diner

   _____

4. a rich, snobbish woman living during the Victorian Age in England

   _____

5. the high school's star athlete (male or female)

   _____

6. the leader of a gang (male or female)

   _____

7. a one-room schoolhouse teacher living during the early part of the 1900's
   (male or female)_____

8. the Chief Executive Officer of a major industrial corporation (male or female)

   _____

9. an angry, mean, and selfish old person (male or female)

   _____

10. a superhero (male or female)

    _____

154.   THE NAMES OF LITERARY CHARACTERS

Authors generally take great care in naming their characters. Often the character's name suggests personality traits and/or other characteristics of the literary figure. Thus, the simple names Snow White and Ebenezer Scrooge give the reader suggestions about the characters even without initially knowing much about them. To many readers, Snow White sounds pure and dainty and Ebenezer Scrooge sounds gruff and unpleasant.

Here are the names of ten literary characters, some better known than others. In the space next to the name, write what personality traits the name suggests to the reader. Then check to see if your assessments match the character's personality as seen in the story.

1. Prince Charming (from the folk tale "Sleeping Beauty")

   _____

   _____

2. Solomon Grundy (from the nursery rhyme "Solomon Grundy")

   _____

   _____

3. Ichabod Crane (from the short story "The Legend of Sleepy Hollow" by Washington Irving)_____

   _____

4. Brom Bones (from the short story "The Legend of Sleepy Hollow" by Washington Irving)_____

   _____

5. Framton Nuttel (from the short story "The Open Window" by Saki)

   _____

   _____

6. James Dillingham Young (from the short story "The Gift of the Magi" by O. Henry)

   _____

   _____

7. Little Bo-Peep (from the nursery rhyme of the same name)

   _____

   _____

8. Rip Van Winkle (from the Washington Irving short story of the same name)

   _____

   _____

9. Tweedledee and Tweedledum (from Lewis Carroll's children's tale *Through the Looking Glass*) _____

   _____

10. Humpty Dumpty (from the Mother Goose nursery rhyme of the same name)

   _____

   _____

155. FAMOUS LITERARY CHARACTERS

Twenty-nine famous literary names are the answers to this crossword puzzle. Some are names you will recall from earlier years and some from more recent readings. Fill in the names and enjoy!

© 1998 by John Wiley & Sons, Inc

ACROSS

1. Becky Thatcher's boyfriend
5. Doyle's detective Sherlock
6. taught Oliver how to pick a pocket or two
10. Barrie's famous flyer
12. Stowe's famous uncle
13. Ernest Lawrence Thayer's famous strike-out victim
15. Tarzan's woman
18. Holmes's friend
19. Stoker's vampire
20. captain in *Moby Dick* by Herman Melville
21. Sewell's famous horse
22. her shoe was fitting for the prince
23. Shelley's monster

DOWN

1. teaches Peter Pan to fly
2. *A Christmas Carol's* miser who saw the true meaning of Christmas
3. A.A. Milne's bear
4. Juliet's man
5. Jekyll's other half
6. Twain's Huckleberry
7. Swift's travelling doctor
8. Porter's optimistic female
9. Ichabod Crane's nemesis
10. Collodi's puppet
11. crippled boy in "A Christmas Carol"
12. Robin Hood's faithful friar
14. Brunhoff's famous elephant
16. "Open sesame" was his famous quote
17. long-haired fairy tale female
20. Lewis Carroll's most famous literary creation

156. SHAKING UP SHAKESPEARE

No book dealing with the English language is complete without a page dedicated to William Shakespeare, probably the world's most famous writer. Whether the work is a tragedy, comedy or history play, if it is by Shakespeare, it is probably read and studied by many people. Rattle Shakespeare's bones by showing him how much you know about his work. Fill in the missing word from each play's title.

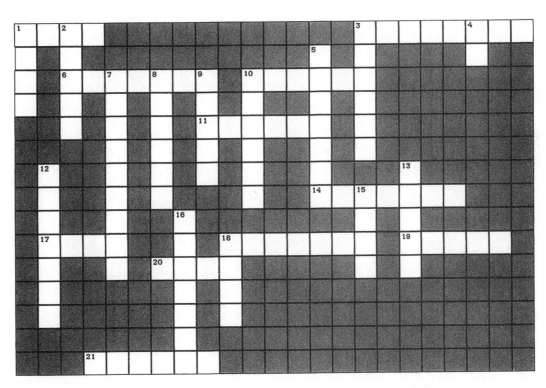

ACROSS

1. Love's Labour's _____
3. The Tragedy of Troilus and _____
6. The Tragedy of King _____ the Second
10. The Merchant of _____
11. The Comedy of _____
14. Much Ado About _____
17. The Tragedy of Othello, the _____ of Venice
18. The Merry Wives of _____
19. The Third Part of King _____ the Sixth
20. The Winter's _____
21. The Tragedy of Romeo and _____

DOWN

1. The Tragedy of King _____
2. The Taming of the _____
3. The Tragedy of Julius _____
4. As You Like _____
5. The Two Noble _____
7. The Tragedy of Antony and _____
8. The Life of Timon of _____
9. A Midsummer Night's _____
10. Two Gentlemen of _____
12. The Tragedy of Hamlet, Prince of _____
13. Twelfth _____
15. Pericles, Prince of _____
16. Measure for _____
18. All's Well That Ends _____

157. AUTHORS OF POPULAR BOOKS FOR TEENS MAGIC SQUARE

Sixteen authors who wrote books that teens have enjoyed are waiting to be matched with their literary creations. Match the author with his or her book. Write your answers in the Magic Square below. Thus, when you match Steinbeck (letter A) with his literary work, that book's assigned number will be placed in the A space within the Magic Square. If your answers are correct, all columns and rows will add up to the same number.

A. STEINBECK
B. ZINDEL
C. LIPSYTE
D. BONHAM

E. SPERRY
F. VOIGHT
G. KNOWLES
H. BAUM

I. GEORGE
J. LONDON
K. ORWELL
L. DICKENS

M. LEE
N. FOX
O. TAYLOR
P. HEMINGWAY

1. The Homecoming
2. Julie of the Wolves
3. Roll of Thunder, Hear My Cry
4. Durango Street
5. To Kill a Mockingbird
6. The Pigman
7. The Wizard of Oz
8. Animal Farm

9. One Fat Summer
10. The Old Man and the Sea
11. The Call of the Wild
12. Call It Courage
13. A Christmas Carol
14. A Separate Peace
15. Of Mice and Men
16. The Slave Dancer

A	B	C	D
E	F	G	H
I	J	K	L
M	N	O	P

158. AUTHORS OF POPULAR NOVELS FOR TEENAGERS CROSSWORD PUZZLE

Twenty-seven books that are teenage favorites are the clues in this puzzle. Write the author's name in the appropriate spaces.

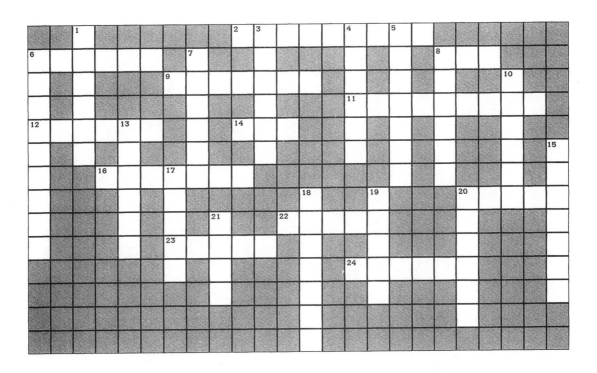

ACROSS

2. Of Mice and Men
6. Call It Courage
8. To Kill a Mockingbird
9. One Fat Summer
11. The Old Man and the Sea
12. The Homecoming
14. The Slave Dancer
16. A Separate Peace
20. Sing Down the Moon
22. Winnie-the-Pooh
23. The Adventures of Tom Sawyer
24. Julie of the Wolves

DOWN

1. A Wizard of Earthsea
3. Roll of Thunder, Hear My Cry
4. Durango Street
5. The Chocolate War
6. Treasure Island
7. The Pigman
8. The Call of the Wild
10. Peter Pan
13. The Outsiders
15. The Princess Bride
17. The Sword in the Stone
18. A Christmas Carol
19. Flowers for Algernon
20. Animal Farm
21. The Wizard of Oz

159. FINDING THE TITLES OF FAMOUS LITERARY WORKS

Thirty-three titles of famous literary works share one thing in common in this activity. Each is missing its last word. Fill in the missing word to complete each title. The number in parentheses indicates the number of letters in the missing word. Then circle the word in the Word Find Puzzle. Words are placed backwards, forward, diagonally, and up and down.

```
F Z B W S T W K N S M S W H R Q P N F T P D O P
S R L Z W O I Y R R R B S Y A C E W G L P L T K
U N O W I A L I C E C A E P B M R A F R H R S P
M B R M N W D D E B Y I A M O D B Q O S A G I H
M W A Q E Z O T I M D W T W A L C U I W N V R V
E J C M V B E N D E T J A I E D D F R I V L C W
R B M R O K R N D M R E S S E N S D S G L B P T
H L H B S H A O Q E P L R R C S I X X A E T Z J
G B Z U K L I Q O R R T B A M X Q H M Z D R H G
T N M F S N T C P K S L K P B N C S C F T T B H
J D C I F X L G A L L N A M W I S T Q A C D P Q
S M G X J Q W V R N L Y S N R V T H K P M F M J
Y L R N V R B F H F S W N F D N N H B G S Z L J
Y J B W H J D Q K S J B F D G Z K B I Z S N B R
D F M Z F D H M L R K M F S L K J V D A Y Z R P
F J P X L W N R Z N G Z Q K G V N K S B K N L L
Y B G F H H T D Z N G T D P Z Z T N B Q S J D T
```

A Christmas _____ (5)

A Day No Pigs Would _____ (3)

A Night to _____ (8)

A Separate _____ (5)

A Tale of Two _____ (6)

A Tree Grows in_____ (8)

Alice's Adventures in _____ (10)

All Things Great and _____ (5)

Animal_____ (4)

Anne of Green _____ (6)

Bridge to _____ (10)

Call of the _____ (4)

Catcher in the _____ (3)

Dandelion _____ (4)

Death Be Not_____ (5)

Ethan _____ (5)

Go Ask _____ (5)

I Know Why the Caged Bird_____ (5)

Little _____(5)

My Darling, My _____(9)

One Fat _____(6)

Rumble _____(4)

Summer of My German _____(7)

That Was Then, This Is _____(3)

The Adventures of Tom _____(6)

The Chocolate _____(3)

The Count of Monte_____(6)

The Hunchback of Notre _____(4)

The Last of the_____(8)

The Old Man and the _____(3)

The Three _____(10)

The Time _____(7)

Treasure_____(6)

160. FAMOUS WOMEN AUTHORS

Twenty famous literary writings by twenty famous women authors are found in this activity. Place the letter of the correct author in the blank next to the number.

1. _____ *Diary of a Young Girl*
   A. Hellman   B. Austen   C. Alcott   D. Frank

2. _____ *Pride and Prejudice*
   A. Austen   B. Smith   C. Shelley   D. Alcott

3. _____ *Little Women*
   A. Angelou   B. Alcott   C. Hansberry   D. Walker

4. _____ *Gone With the Wind*
   A. Austen   B. Mitchell   C. Porter   D. Chopin

5. _____ *A Raisin in the Sun*
   A. O'Connor   B. Cather   C. Hansberry   D. Angelou

6. _____ *Their Eyes Were Watching God*
   A. Frank   B. Austen   C. Hurston   D. Plath

7. _____ *The Story of My Life*
   A. Keller   B. Angelou   C. Mitchell   D. Dinesen

8. _____ *Ethan Frome*
   A. Shelley   B. Hurston   C. Woolf   D. Wharton

9. _____ *Ship of Fools*
   A. Porter   B. Eliot   C. Hurston   D. Chopin

10. _____ *Frankenstein*
    A. Shelley   B. Lee   C. McCullers   D. O'Connor

11. _____ *The Awakening*
    A. Woolf   B. Hellman   C. Walker   D. Chopin

12. _____ *A Tree Grows in Brooklyn*
    A. Smith   B. Frank   C. Browning   D. Buck

13. _____ *Middlemarch*
    A. Stowe   B. Eliot   C. Plath   D. Wharton

14. _____ *Out of Africa*
    A. Dinesen   B. Woolf   C. Morrison   D. Walker

15. _____ *The Bluest Eye*
    A. Keller   B. Wharton   C. Morrison   D. Angelou

16. _____ *The Color Purple*
    A. Alcott   B. Porter   C. Walker   D. Brooks

17. _____ *To the Lighthouse*
    A. Woolf   B. Buck   C. Rawlings   D. Stein

18. _____ *To Kill a Mockingbird*
    A. Lee   B. Keller   C. McCullers   D. Frank

19. _____ *Uncle Tom's Cabin*
    A. Woolf   B. Hurston   C. Shelley   D. Stowe

20. _____ *I Know Why the Caged Bird Sings*
    A. Frank   B. Angelou   C. Hellman   D. Smith

Name _____ Date _____ Period _____

161. THINKING ABOUT BOOKS

Here is your chance to think about what you have read. Characters, settings, scenes, controversial issues and more will be considered in this informal reading survey. Answer the questions in the spaces provided and then discuss your answers with your classmates.

1. Who is one of the most memorable characters you have encountered in your reading? _____ Why? _____
_____

2. Who is a character who reminded you of someone you know? _____
Why? _____

3. Recount an exciting scene you remember from your reading. _____
_____
_____

4. Which book would you say is a "must read" for someone your age? _____
_____ Why? _____

5. Which book has a good beginning? _____ Why is it a good
beginning? _____
_____

6. A memorable family is found in which book? _____
This family is memorable because _____

7. A book that made you see something in a new way is _____
What did you see in a new way? _____
How was your opinion changed? _____

8. Which book included a controversial issue? _____
What was the controversial issue? _____

9. A humorous scene is found in the book _____
Summarize the funny scene in a few lines. _____
_____
_____

10. A book that had a good ending is _____
Summarize why the ending is good. _____
_____
_____

162. ARE WE WHAT WE READ?

You have probably heard the expression, "You are what you eat." Well, here's today's question. "Are we what we read?" By looking at the reading habits of the reading public, we might be able to make some assumptions about what interests us. Can we assume that because we buy a book about something that we have an interest in that subject matter? If so, then perhaps we are what we read. Are we heavily into science fiction? Do we read many self-help books? Why do we like to read about the lives of celebrities?

Using a Best Sellers List, available in many libraries and newspapers, make some generalizations about the types of books that interest us. Do the topics we read about in fiction books differ from those in the nonfiction books we read? How? What types of books have been on the Best Sellers List for an extended period of time? Why? In the space below write your findings about the types of books we purchase and read.

_____

_____

_____

_____

_____

_____

_____

_____

_____

_____

_____

_____

_____

163. WHAT KIND OF READER ARE YOU?

It is interesting to take a look at your reading habits to see exactly what kind of reader you are. Here are some questions that will help you assess yourself as a reader. Answer the questions as specifically as you can and then discuss the results with your teacher and classmates. After you have exchanged these reading ideas, look for ways in which you can improve your reading.

1. What types of reading materials interest you (magazines, biographies, newspapers, novels, plays, short stories, poems, others)? _____
_____

2. Is most of your reading for pleasure or required reading? _____

3. Do you have a favorite place in which you do your reading (library, bedroom, den, other)?
_____

4. How does your reading differ if you have to read a required school assignment as opposed to your reading for pleasure? _____
_____

5. Are there any types of reading materials that you have little or no interest in (science-fiction, fashion, sports, other)? _____
_____

6. Do you try to improve the speed of your reading? _____

7. If your answer to question 6 is "yes," how do you try to improve your speed?_____
_____

8. Other than the time spent reading school assignments, how much time do you spend each day reading? _____

9. Do you read more during the summer months or during the school year? _____
_____

10. Do you recommend anything you have read to others? _____

11. What benefits are derived from reading? _____
_____

12. Do you think that when you become an adult you will read more or less than you do now? _____ Why? _____

Section Seven

THE EVERYDAY USE OF OUR LANGUAGE

164. A HERCULEAN TASK

You won't have to be as strong as Hercules, but you will have to know who he was in order to answer question 21 across correctly. Since a Herculean task is one difficult to accomplish, the word Herculean fits as the correct answer to that clue. All of the other clues deal with **eponyms**, words named after real or mythical people and places. So dig in and make Hercules cower with your brain power!

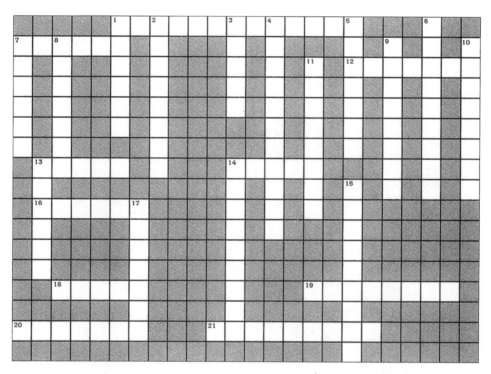

ACROSS

1. political principle based on craftiness and expediency
7. to make incoherent sounds
12. warlike
13. book of maps
14. of great size or strength
16. handsome young man
18. device used to produce a loud sound
19. completely sealed
20. a costly victory
21. word describing a difficult task to accomplish

DOWN

1. trusted guide; tutor
2. type of sweater
3. a very beautiful woman
4. very small
5. one who is the enemy of another
6. fond of luxury and expense
7. place of noise and confusion
8. to refuse to buy, or sell, or use
9. type of psychology
10. women's undergarments
11. relationship based on spiritual and intellectual considerations
13. woman warrior
14. to tease by showing something one will withhold
15. quick; quick-witted; volatile
17. devilish or wicked

165. REVIEW OF REAL AND FICTIONAL PEOPLE, PLACES, AND THINGS

Here are twenty-five people, places, and things, some real, some fictional, whose names have become part of our language. Midas, an ancient king, gave us the expression, "Midas touch." Match these names with their descriptions. Write your number answers in the magic squares below. When your answers are correct, all columns and rows add up to the same number.

A	B	C	D	E
F	G	H	I	J
K	L	M	N	O
P	Q	R	S	T
U	V	W	X	Y

A. FREUDIAN
B. BOYCOTT
C. BLOOMERS
D. ADONIS
E. TANTALIZE
F. NEMESIS
G. SATANIC
H. LILLIPUTIAN
I. BEDLAM
J. SIREN
K. TITAN
L. VENUS
M. HERCULEAN
N. CARDIGAN
O. BABBLE
P. MARTIAL
Q. ATLAS
R. HERMETIC
S. PYRRHIC
T. PLATONIC
U. AMAZON
V. EPICUREAN
W. MERCURIAL
X. MACHIAVELLIAN
Y. MENTOR

1. type of psychology
2. quick; quick-witted; volatile
3. relationship based on spiritual and intellectual considerations
4. a very beautiful woman
5. place of noise and confusion
6. political principle based on craftiness and expediency
7. warlike
8. word describing a difficult task to accomplish
9. device used to produce a loud sound
10. to refuse to buy, or sell, or use
11. very small
12. to tease by showing something one will withhold
13. fond of luxury and expense
14. a costly victory
15. of great size or strength
16. book of maps
17. type of sweater
18. one who is the enemy of another
19. women's undergarments
20. trusted guide; tutor
21. to make incoherent sounds
22. devilish or wicked
23. handsome young man
24. woman warrior
25. completely sealed

166. DOCTOR, DOCTOR!

The names of sixteen different types of doctors are hidden in this word search puzzle. Clues indicating each doctor's specialty and the names of the sixteen doctors can help you find the doctors' names which are placed backwards, forward, diagonally, and up and down. The number in parentheses indicates the number of letters in the doctor's name.

```
L C C B R R N N T P S V V J Z V Z D M C W P E X
F G H X R K G B E S S P J B G N L E V D R L N M
R N I C B Z K H C U F Y N F M D T N M P R A D Y
V G R B N D U Z T W R Q C S P S B T L T D S O Y
T P O D I A T R I S T O P H I L N I T K T T D F
W P P W L L I B O M I C L G I A L S V S S I O C
Y V R S S L W C Q L W G O O I A I T I Q I C N Y
J X A B X E K K I P O L O R G G T G N J G S T V
F Z C F R R B G J R O G A L O I O R N Z O U I F
Y W T R Y G B M B M T N I L O L S N I C L R S L
X F O Y H I X Y L R I A O S O I Q T C S O G T G
B H R Z Y S S A J R Q H I H T D D Z T J T E M L
T T D W H T H F E Q T S C D Q T P R C X A O G C
J H S H W T H T S A Q Y L Z E Y C J A Q M N B T
V G W Q H J E W P N S B T S S P G L S C R J R N
N M Z P N V Y C R P G C Q G F B T T V P E D P Z
D K O G P S K J K M F G J K F M L B C V D F M H
```

animals (12)

eyes (15)

feet (10)

heart (12)

hypersensitivity to specific
  substances (9)

infants and children (12)

manipulation of body joints,
  especially the spine (12)

mind and mental and emotional
  processes (12)

mind disorders (12)

nature of diseases (11)

nervous system (11)

reparation of injured or
  deformed body parts (14)

root canal therapy (11)

skin (13)

teeth (7)

urinary system (9)

ALLERGIST	DERMATOLOGIST	PATHOLOGIST	PSYCHIATRIST
CARDIOLOGIST	ENDODONTIST	PEDIATRICIAN	PSYCHOLOGIST
CHIROPRACTOR	NEUROLOGIST	PLASTIC SURGEON	UROLOGIST
DENTIST	OPHTHALMOLOGIST	PODIATRIST	VETERINARIAN

167. EXPRESSIONS USING BODY PARTS

If you have ever given a movie a "thumb's down" or had to "shake a leg," you will understand the idea of this puzzle. Match the expressions in Column A with their meanings in Column B. Be "on your toes" and go "head over heels" for this activity!

Column A		**Column B**
1. _____	bite one's lip	A. submit
2. _____	turn a deaf ear	B. fool another
3. _____	head for	C. influenced greatly by another
4. _____	win by a neck	D. give as inheritance
5. _____	pull his leg	E. be victorious by a slim margin
6. _____	on one's toes	F. without grace
7. _____	hand down	G. try hard
8. _____	go back on	H. near exhaustion or death
9. _____	lift a finger	I. to keep back one's anger
10. _____	shake a leg	J. sneakily
11. _____	on his last legs	K. alert
12. _____	with a heavy hand	L. make a slight effort
13. _____	hand in	M. hurry
14. _____	behind one's back	N. follow orders
15. _____	show one's hand	O. show your intentions
16. _____	thumb's down	P. signal of rejection
17. _____	break one's neck	Q. go in that direction
18. _____	toe the line	R. completely
19. _____	under one's thumb	S. betray
20. _____	head over heels	T. pay no attention to

168. FIRST NAMES AND BODY PARTS

If your teacher asks you to "mark your book's appendix," you have an idea of what this activity is all about. The word **mark** is a person's first name and a verb meaning "to note." The word **appendix** is a body part and the name for a book's section. Each of this puzzle's answers is either a person's first name or a body part that also has another meaning. So if you have an eye and a nose for some fun, you have come to the right place! Write the answers in the correct spaces.

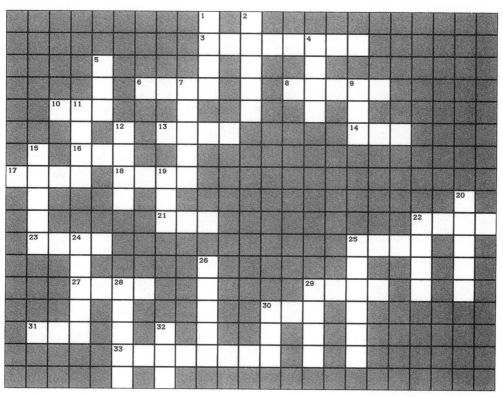

ACROSS

3. supplementary material at the end of a book
6. needed to fix a car's flat
8. essence or core
10. weapon
13. wealthy
14. move up and down
16. bring civil action against
17. prow of a ship
18. young cow
21. to tap
22. twelve inches
23. end of a loaf of bread
25. *Gone With the Wind's* setting
27. to support
29. banana cluster
30. threading hole in a needle
31. mechanical closing part of a vise
33. edge of a paved road

DOWN

1. grade
2. month before May
4. past tense of draw
5. chewing substance
7. high, steep grade of rock
9. to kid or tease
11. past tense of rise
12. narrowest part of a bottle
15. part of a saw, fork or comb
19. projecting rim of a pitcher
20. front opening in the gun's barrel
22. surface of a card or clock
24. to form an angle
25. clapper of a bell
26. song
28. public fund
29. leader
30. unit of corn
32. to wear

169. CLICKING WITH CLICHÉS

Clichés are defined as overused expressions. When someone is described as being "as light as a feather," he or she is described with a cliché. Match the last word of each cliché. Then write the answers in the Magic Square below. Thus, if the answer to question #1 is *nails*, letter O, should be placed in the same box. Match each cliché with its last word. Your answers are correct if all columns and rows add up to the same number.

A. WINK
B. DAISY
C. WORD
D. HOUSE

E. RUG
F. ARROW
G. HILLS
H. GOLD

I. DOORNAIL
J. FEATHER
K. BEE
L. BELL

M. ICE
N. RAIL
O. NAILS
P. CUCUMBER

1. as tough as _____
2. as big as a _____
3. as light as a _____
4. as snug as a bug in a _____
5. as dead as a _____
6. as straight as an _____
7. as cool as a _____
8. as good as my _____

9. as good as _____
10. as busy as a _____
11. as quick as a _____
12. as skinny as a _____
13. as fresh as a _____
14. as cold as _____
15. as old as the _____
16. as clear as a _____

A	B	C	D
E	F	G	H
I	J	K	L
M	N	O	P

170. WIN BROWNIE POINTS AND EARN ADVANCEMENT!

"Brownie points" is a cliché or an overused expression. It was originally a term used by the Brownies, part of the Girl Scouts of America, to win merit points. Winning is the essence of the quote that you will find if you have correctly matched the clichés in Column A with their meanings in Column B. Write the two-letter answers in the spaces next to the appropriate numbers and then again (in the same order) on the line after the last question. In this way you will spell out the quote and its speaker. Good luck.

Column A		Column B
1. ____ below the belt	(at)	to deny responsibility for
2. ____ change one's tune	(ct)	leave it as is
3. ____ chew the fat	(ea)	bribe
4. ____ easy as pie	(eg)	do business
5. ____ feast or famine	(er)	bright
6. ____ grease one's palms	(il)	reverse one's stance
7. ____ hit the nail on the head	(iw)	behavior that is unfair
8. ____ in the bag	(la)	get to the point exactly
9. ____ leave well enough alone	(le)	very happy
10. ____ mark my words	(ln)	talk informally
11. ____ never say die	(nd)	do something in a set way
12. ____ on cloud nine	(or)	listen well
13. ____ play with fire	(ot)	not difficult
14. ____ run like clockwork	(re)	to speak in an ironic manner
15. ____ sharp as a tack	(st)	much more or much less than needed
16. ____ spic and span	(th)	very clean
17. ____ talk turkey	(vi)	a surety
18. ____ tongue-in-cheek	(xa)	put oneself in danger
19. ____ wash one's hands of	(ya)	don't give up

The quote and the speaker are _____

_____.

171. AVOID THE CLICHÉS

Clichés, overused expressions, are found too frequently in writing. This activity will help identify those expressions that should be avoided in formal writing. Match the first part of the cliché found in Column A with its last word found in Column B. Write the correct letter in the appropriate space next to the matching number. If your answers are correct, the answers will spell out a piece of advice for you concerning clichés. Write out that message on the line under the last question.

Column A	Column B
1. ___ clear as a _____	a. bell
2. ___ famous last _____	c. sky
3. ___ get under one's _____	c. cakes
4. ___ have a nice _____	d. Joneses
5. ___ keep up with the _____	e. moon
6. ___ light as a _____	e. degree
7. ___ in the nick of _____	h. time
8. ___ once in a blue _____	h. thunder
9. ___ pie in the _____	i. day
10. ___ put two and two_____	i. ready
11. ___ rough and _____	l. together
12. ___ sell like hot _____	o. skin
13. ___ steal someone's _____	s. thinking
14. ___ to get the third _____	t. feather
15. ___ wishful _____	v. words

The message found in the answer column is_____.

172. DON'T GET CAUGHT BETWEEN A ROCK AND A HARD PLACE

The expression "caught between a rock and a hard place" means to be in an undesirable position. This activity will test your knowledge of idioms. Here are twenty common idioms in the language. Using the words from the list below, select the correct word needed to complete the idiom. Starting with answer number one, each set of three consecutive answers shares a common theme. Write each theme on the appropriate lines below question 15.

back	egg	pie
bacon	eye	red
bed	green	shirt
boots	hats	wall
closet	leg	yellow

1. Jerry lost his _____ in the card game at Hank's house.
2. All night he was so scared that he would lose over $2,000 that he was shivering in his _____.
3. On other occasions Jerry's opponents could tip their _____ to him for he played so well.
4. Jerry thought he would beat those players and bring home the _____.
5. Thinking he was so much better than they, he thought winning would be as easy as _____.
6. He had _____ on his face after he had been trounced so badly in the game.
7. The other players' kidding throughout the night was driving Jerry up the _____.
8. He felt that this night might be a skeleton in the _____ and hoped that the other players would not tell too many other people about his bad night.
9. His mood after the game seemed as though he had gotten up on the wrong side of the _____.
10. On previous card game nights, Jerry had lost a little money and it was no sweat off his _____.
11. He thought with all his card playing experience he would have a _____ up on the other less experienced players.
12. To augment his income Jerry would always keep an _____ out for a card game in the area.
13. On some other nights Jerry had won so much money that the other players were _____ with envy.
14. They were seeing _____ after Jerry had won so much of their money.
15. Yet, after losing so much tonight, Jerry wondered if he would turn into a _____ belly and be afraid to play in future card games.

Common theme for 1–3 _____
Common theme for 4–6 _____
Common theme for 7–9 _____
Common theme for 10–12 _____
Common theme for 13–15 _____

© 1998 by John Wiley & Sons, Inc

173. THIS IS SUCH SWEET SORROW

"Sweet sorrow" is an example of an **oxymoron**, a figure of speech that combines contradictory ideas or terms. The two-word oxymorons in this activity have been split up with the first word of the oxymoron in Column A and its second word in Column B. Match the two words of each oxymoron by writing the correct letter next to each number. Your answer column will feature a boy's name, a type of fish, and a witty remark.

Column A	Column B
1. _____ clearly	a. news
2. _____ cruel	b. vacation
3. _____ definite	c. gas
4. _____ eloquent	d. creamer
5. _____ genuine	e. imitation
6. _____ good	f. games
7. _____ home	g. confused
8. _____ jumbo	h. curve
9. _____ linear	i. live
10. _____ liquid	j. secret
11. _____ nonalcoholic	k. silence
12. _____ nondairy	l. shrimp
13. _____ old	m. kindness
14. _____ open	n. grief
15. _____ passively	o. beer
16. _____ randomly	p. silence
17. _____ same	q. organized
18. _____ taped	r. maybe
19. _____ thunderous	s. aggressive
20. _____ war	t. office
21. _____ working	u. difference

The boy's name is _____. The type of fish is _____.

The witty remark is _____.

174. SHAKE A LEG AND POUR YOUR HEART OUT

These ten questions concern idiomatic expressions, words joined together that are not taken literally. So when someone says he has had a "change of heart," don't think he has undergone a heart transplant. "Shake a leg" and "pour your heart out" are two idioms that you will encounter in this activity. Circle the correct answer and then write the letter in the space. If your answers are correct, they will spell out the first three words of another idiom. What is that idiom's last word? Write it in the space below question 10.

1. _____ To remain out of debt, you (t) keep your head above water, or (u) tickle your ribs.

2. _____ One who is poor lives (g) with his head in the clouds, or (h) from hand to mouth.

3. _____ When you are in a hurry, you (r) shake a leg, or (q) keep your nose clean.

4. _____ When you can't quite remember something, it is (o) on the tip of your tongue, or (p) highway robbery.

5. _____ Roberto soon forgot what his mother told him. His mother's words (v) came clean, or (w) went in one ear and out the other.

6. _____ Since Vicky felt that she made a fool of herself, she (i) had egg on her face, or (j) was clear as a bell.

7. _____ Things that are plentiful and readily available are (m) highway robbery, or (n) a dime a dozen.

8. _____ Kerrie fell asleep. She went (t) to the land of Nod, or (u) poured out her heart.

9. _____ One who wants to be forgiven is often (h) on bended knee, or (l) making neither hide nor hair of something.

10. _____ A trusted friend is your (d) mother tongue, or (e) right arm.

The idiom (including its last word) is _____.

© 1998 by John Wiley & Sons, Inc

175. EXPRESSIONS

The underlined words are some common expressions in our language. In the space below the sentence write the expression's meaning. The first is done for you.

1. <u>Keep an eye on</u> your younger brother while I go into the store.
   Watch him _____

2. That noise is <u>driving me up the wall</u>.

   _____

3. With my <u>ear to the ground</u>, I tried to find the answer.

   _____

4. The science lecture was <u>over his head</u>.

   _____

5. When it came to working with his hands, he was <u>all thumbs</u>.

   _____

6. The coach told us that even though we had not done well in the first half, we should <u>keep our chins up</u>.

   _____

7. In order for him to be in that position, he had to <u>step on someone's toes</u>.

   _____

8. Jocelyn loved <u>to rub elbows with</u> the celebrities on the set.

   _____

9. Penny <u>got her back up</u> when she heard the news from the meeting.

   _____

10. This new assignment was <u>no bed of roses</u> for the experienced policeman.

    _____

11. Fred warned Timmy that if he really wanted to know the truth, he should <u>read between the lines</u>.

    _____

12. Reggie had <u>an ax to grind</u> after the most recent meeting with his colleague.

    _____

13. The <u>dark horse</u> in the presidential race seemed to be taking the lead.

    _____

14. Each of the participants knew that the contest would be <u>a hard row to hoe</u>.

    _____

15. The mentor kept in mind the fact that <u>birds of a feather</u> flock together.

    _____

176. MORE EXPRESSIONS

In the space provided below each sentence, write the meaning of the underlined expression.

1. The <u>cat is out of the bag</u> now!

   _____

2. We could easily tell that the boss <u>got up on the wrong side of the bed</u>.

   _____

3. The store manager wanted everything to be <u>spic and span</u> for the new season.

   _____

4. Unfortunately, we've seen <u>neither hide nor hair</u> of her since she left the building yesterday.

   _____

5. Our family never felt the need <u>to keep up with the Joneses</u>.

   _____

6. From the moment he first saw Maureen, he was <u>head over heels</u> in love with her.

   _____

7. Every time we play our rival school, the game is <u>nip and tuck</u>.

   _____

8. The guilty members of the class knew that it was now time <u>to face the music</u>.

   _____

9. The man was given the <u>keys to the city</u>.

   _____

10. She knew that she would win the prize <u>by hook or by crook</u>.

    _____

11. All of us realized that he was <u>crying crocodile tears</u>.

    _____

12. We stayed after the game and <u>shot the bull</u> for a while.

    _____

13. Ginny was always <u>the apple of his eye</u>.

    _____

14. Vince should have realized that he would <u>pay through the nose</u>.

    _____

15. That victory was a real <u>feather in his cap</u>.

    _____

177. PUTTING PROVERBS IN THEIR PROPER PLACES

A proverb is a short saying that expresses an obvious truth. Vanessa's mother is beautiful and intelligent. So is Vanessa. Looking at the two women, one might remark, "The fruit doesn't fall too far from the tree." This saying is a proverb that befits the situation since the mother and the daughter (analogously the tree and the fruit) are much the same. Thus, the proverb is appropriate to the situation.

Here are eight proverbs. Similar to the situation involving Vanessa and her mother, create a situation that befits the proverb. Write your situation on the lines next to the proverb.

1. Curiosity killed the cat. _____

_____

2. You don't know what you've got until it's gone. _____

_____

3. Better late than never. _____

_____

4. All's well that ends well. _____

_____

5. To err is human; to forgive, divine. _____

_____

6. If the shoe fits, wear it. _____

_____

7. Patience is a virtue. _____

_____

8. Still water runs deep. _____

_____

178. WORDS THAT HAVE I AS THEIR SECOND LETTER

Each of these twenty-five words feature the letter *i* as its second letter. Let that letter help you fill in correct words for these clues.

ACROSS

1. the circumference of a tree
3. to separate into parts
4. conversation between two or more
6. to imitate
8. evil
10. agile
12. to steal small sums or objects
14. politeness
16. to dry up
17. space between rows
19. occurring every two years
20. musical instrument

DOWN

2. break or rest
3. lessen
4. instructive
5. to make light ringing sounds
6. joy or merriment
7. widespread
9. slight trace
11. two-footed animal
13. something imagined
14. fortress
15. small boat
16. stubborn
18. to start

179. TWO ON THE AISLE

The ideal location for a seat in the theater usually includes the phrase, "two on the aisle." Here are twenty-three terms used in the theater and theatrical productions. Fill in the correct answers to these clues below.

ACROSS

1. one who performs in a play
3. scenery for a play
8. action in a story
9. sound qualities of a room
12. those attending the play
15. form of literature known as plays
17. acting platform
18. theater employee who shows people to their seats
19. wicked or evil character

DOWN

2. clothes worn by the performers
3. setting of the play
4. serious play with a unhappy ending
5. a soliloquy
6. disagreement
7. author of the drama
8. main character in the play
9. a segment of a play
10. person in a play
11. chief role in the play
13. conversation between the actors
14. turning point
16. practice performance
17. growing excitement

180. SOME FUN WITH WORDS

Here is a game you're sure to enjoy. Each answer is made up of two words that rhyme. So if you were asked for the telegraph line inventor Samuel's steeds, the answer is "Morse's horses." Fill in the two-word answer next to the question.

1. _____ President Roosevelt's regulars

2. _____ Executed spy's stories

3. _____ *Uncle Tom's Cabin's* author's troubles

4. _____ Franklin's desires

5. _____ Midnight rider's hearing organs

6. _____ Slave rebellion leader Nat's pupils

7. _____ President Bush's fake signatures

8. _____ Depression president's windows

9. _____ Cotton gin inventor's small cars

10. _____ Model T producer's ropes

11. _____ Tippecanoe's soldiers

12. _____ *The Story of My Life* author's basements

13. _____ Famous Louisiana senator's misdeeds

14. _____ *War of the Worlds'* Orson's beauties

15. _____ First American in orbit's marshes

16. _____ First female American in space's travels

17. _____ Supreme Court Justice David's fans

18. _____ President Eisenhower's long walks

19. _____ Civil Right's leader King's cardboard boxes

20. _____ President Clinton's medical tablets

181. ANIMALS IN THE LANGUAGE

The names of various animals are found often in our everyday speech. For instance, *a dog-eat-dog world* is an expression signifying how tough the world can be. Since each answer contains the name of an animal, this puzzle tests your knowledge of the different ways in which animals find their way into our language. Fill in the correct letters within the puzzle.

ACROSS

2. to put up with
3. anxious
5. to hit with a wooden object
7. to peddle goods by shouting
9. to treat as a celebrity
11. symbol for peace
12. to imitate another
13. a golf score of two under par
15. slang term for a sports referee
16. as dumb as an __
17. to get out of the way
18. stubborn; obstinate
19. a favorable position

DOWN

1. a short rest
2. sluggish; slow, dull, stupid
4. to move, curve, or twist
5. rising
6. quiet and timid
8. a type of mock court
9. a children's game
10. huge
11. to follow or hunt another
14. to nag one's husband

182. WHY DON'T YOU LOOK IN THE NEWSPAPER?

"What will the temperature be next Tuesday when we go to Toronto?" This is a typical question you might have before making a trip. With so much information on so many different topics, a newspaper can give us the answer to this question. Listed below are the sections in a typical newspaper; immediately following are questions that can be answered by using a newspaper. In the space next to each question, write the letter of the section in which the answer to the question can be found.

Each letter is used only once.

Sections

(a) Business (finance and world markets)

(b) Classifieds (employment opportunities)

(c) Comics (cartoons)

(d) Editorials (columnists air their opinions)

(e) Entertainment (television, radio, movies, theater and other arts events)

(f) Letters to the Editor (readers respond to events and articles)

(g) News (international, national, and local news events)

(h) Obituaries (death notices)

(i) Sports (world, national, and local sporting events and news)

(j) Travel (tips on travel opportunities and personal travel experiences)

(k) Weather (world, national, and local weather news)

1. _____ "Are any fast food chains hiring part-time workers this time of year?"

2. _____ "What are the best places to visit in England?"

3. _____ "What movies start around seven-thirty in my area?"

4. _____ "What silly thing will Little Orphan Annie do today?"

5. _____ "In which funeral parlor can I pay my respects for Mr. Thompson?"

6. _____ "Did the Toronto Blue Jays play the Chicago White Sox last night?"

7. _____ "What was William F. Buckley's opinion about the political convention?"

8. _____ "How did the Stock Market do yesterday?"

9. _____ "What was the people's reaction to Mr. Buckley's essay?"

10. _____ "Did the Chinese government react favorably to Canada's decision?"

11. _____ "Will it snow at any time during the next few days around here?"

183. WHAT'S SO SPECIAL ABOUT NTH?

One of the few words in the English language that does not contain a vowel (a,e,i,o,u,or y) is the word *nth*. Here are fifteen other words that end in *th*. The first letter of each word is given to you. Fill in the missing letters.

1. p__th

2. f__ __th

3. b__ __th

4. w__ __th

5. d__ __ __th

6. s__ __ __ __th

7. b__ __ __ __th

8. w__ __ __th

9. h__ __ __th

10. u__ __ __ __th

11. e__ __ __th

12. s__ __th

13. z__ __ __th

14. g__ __th

15. m__ __th

184. HOW THESE WORDS CAME TO BE

Below are the derivations or origins of twenty words. Many of them are quite interesting; others are quite surprising. Place the letter of the matching description in Column B in the appropriate space in front of the number in Column A. The first is already done for you.

Column A	**Column B**
1. __P__ ultimate	A. forty days
2. _____ satellite	B. sphere
3. _____ grain	C. to weigh
4. _____ employ	D. child's nurse
5. _____ knot	E. an attendant
6. _____ orb	F. a fitting
7. _____ differ	G. to bring apart
8. _____ benign	H. to engage
9. _____ judo	I. soft way
10. _____ tenant	J. well-born
11. _____ pensive	K. to draw
12. _____ quarantine	L. to drive
13. _____ manual	M. to boast noisily
14. _____ wheel	N. to press together
15. _____ nun	O. a circle
16. _____ harmony	P. to come to an end
17. _____ attract	Q. hand
18. _____ leper	R. seed or kernel
19. _____ yelp	S. to peel off
20. _____ impel	T. to hold

185. FOREIGN WORDS AND PHRASES

Match the sixteen foreign words and phrases with their definitions. Write your answers in the Magic Square below. If your answers are correct, all columns and rows will total the same number.

A. CARPE DIEM

B. AD INFINITUM

C. SHALOM

D. EX POST FACTO

E. FAUX PAS

F. QUID PRO QUO

G. AD HOC

H. ALOHA

I. SAVOIR FAIRE

J. ENTRE NOUS

K. PER DIEM

L. DEUS EX MACHINA

M. ID EST

N. GLASNOST

O. COUP D'ETAT

P. TETE-A-TETE

1. that is

2. this for that

3. hello or goodbye

4. overthrow of the state

5. god from the machine

6. peace

7. seize the day

8. just between us

9. per day

10. after the fact

11. without end

12. know how

13. openness

14. mistake

15. for a specific purpose

16. head-to-head serious talk

A	B	C	D
E	F	G	H
I	J	K	L
M	N	O	P

186. SPORTS HEADLINES

Sports headlines often make use of the pun in describing the outcome of a sporting event. With words such as swamp, maul, and claw, headline writers use graphic words to describe the result. Twenty verbs are listed in the Word Bank. Paying particularly close attention to the sentence's subject, select the best word to fit each of the twenty headlines and write its letter in the space within the proper headline. Each verb is used only once.

 1. Jets _____ over the Chargers.
 2. Tigers _____ the Chiefs.
 3. Mariners _____ the Yankees.
 4. Angels _____ above the Cardinals.
 5. Rangers _____ the Royals.
 6. Celtics _____ the Knicks.
 7. Clippers_____ the Lakers.
 8. Indians _____ the Twins.
 9. Cowboys _____ the Eagles.
10. Lions _____ over the Dolphins.
11. Hornets _____ the Sixers.
12. Dodgers _____ loss to the Braves.
13. Magic _____ the Rockets.
14. Browns _____ the Falcons.
15. Kings _____ the Canucks.
16. Bulls _____ the Cavaliers.
17. Supersonics _____ the Grizzlies.
18. Oilers _____ the Forty-Niners.
19. Nets _____ the Timberwolves.
20. Heat _____ the Nuggets.

arrest	color	rise	sink
avoid	conquer	roar	soar
baffles	crown	rustle	snare
burns	cut	scalp	stampede
claw	outslick	shatter	sting

APPENDIX

THE INTERNET CONNECTION

- •Authors
- •Education
- •Grammar
- •Language Arts
- •Lesson Plans
- •Literature
- •Research
- •Words
- •Writing

INTERNET SITES FOR ENGLISH TEACHERS

The Internet is a valuable resource for today's English teachers and students. Using the computer to find information has made research more convenient. The following Internet sites and addresses will certainly aid you and your students in many ways. These sites will provide access to literally hundreds of other sites. They have been selected because of their usefulness and merit. Just as importantly, they are channels to other equally informative areas.

The addresses should be typed in exactly as they appear below, excluding the parentheses. After that, the sky's the limit as to where you can wind up. Have fun!

Authors

WebCrawler Arts: Literature features Author Pages at (http://webcrawler.com/select/art.histlit.html). Here is a reader's dream come true. Authors include Austen, Carroll, Faulkner, Hawthorne, Hemingway, Joyce, London, Melville, Shakespeare, and Twain. A wealth of information about their lives, works, criticisms, and other related areas are found here.

In Literary Kicks, Beat Generation Writers including Jack Kerouac and Allen Ginsberg are featured. (http://www.charm.net/~brooklyn/LitKicks.html)

Emily Dickinson fans will love the Dickinson site at (http://lal.cs.byu.edu/people/black/dickinson.html). Links to 440 of her poems, an e-mail discussion group, A Celebration of Women Writers link, and more are found here.

George Bernard Shaw's page (http://www.gis.net/~edwardg/shaw.html) features materials about his life, works, philosophy, and memorable quotes.

The Shakespeare Web (http://www.Shakespeare.com/) will give you more than enough information on the Bard. Many other paths to information on Shakespeare are available through this address.

Another interesting Shakespeare site is Shakespeare Illustrated (http://www.cc.emory.edu/ENGLISH/classes/Shakespeare_Illustrated/Shakespeare.ht). This site explores nineteenth-century painting, criticism, and productions of the Bard's plays. Lists of paintings associated with each play are also here.

Education

The U.S. Department of Education (http://www.ed.gov/) includes information on programs and services, publications and products, selected governmental education programs and initiatives, and applications for educational grants.

EdWeb: The Online K–12 Resource Guide provides useful resources for K–12 teachers—some interactive—including discussion groups, lesson plans, and stories about teaching. (http://webcrawler.com/select/edtech.03.html)

Grammar

Online English Grammar (http://www.edunet.com/english/grammar/index.html.) provides a valuable source for questions dealing with grammar. The site offers a grammar clinic and language practice pages.

Language Arts

Language Arts and Reading Resources (http://206.76.136.3/resources/la.html) is a wealth of information for the English teacher. Information on Children's Literature, Creative Writing on the Internet, Language Arts lesson plans, a National Council of Teachers of English (NCTE) page, National Writing Project, Web Resources for English Teachers, Internet Resources for Special Educators, Resources for Young Writers, and Educational (and Fun) WWW Sites for kids, teachers, and parents are all here.

The Los Angeles Office of Education's site, Language Arts Resources, is a fine site helpful to both Language Arts and Literature teachers. Offered here are Caldecott Awards, California Language Arts SCORE Project, Create Your Own Newspaper, Online Writing Tutorial for students in grades 6, 7, and 8, links to information on authors and their works, Greek myths, Kids' Pub (posting children's own stories), Newberry Awards, and the Online Books Page (over 1,600 English works in various formats). (http://teams.lacoe.edu/documentation/places/language.html)

Lesson Plans

Lesson Plans on the Internet at http://www.swift.cps.k12.il.us/swift/lessons.html is an excellent resource for teachers. Categories including Creating Lesson Plans, Internet Lesson Plans, Language Arts – Lesson Plans, Lesson Plan Archive – AskEric, and Lesson Plans – Colleague Exchange are available at this site.

Literature

American Literature Online (http://www.missouri.edu/~engmo/amlit.html) is a favorite site for both teachers and students of American literature. Pages featuring Native American Lit, Women Writers, African-American Writers, research tools, individual authors, electronic archives home page for teaching American Literature, and other Web resources are available at this site.

English Literature and Composition Resources on the Internet: Selected Sites (http://www.iat.unc.edu/guides/irg-30.html) includes valuable sites for Literature, Composition/Rhetoric, Writing Centers and Laboratories, Dictionaries and Other Tools, and other resources, including new tools for teaching.

Voice of the Shuttle English Literature Main Page (http://humanitas.ucsb.edu/shuttle/english.html) includes works written in English taught in English and American literature departments. Additionally, links to literary texts, Creative Writing, Cultural Studies, and Poetry Studies are featured here.

University of Manitoba English Department (http://www.umanitoba.ca/English/English.html) has links to English Studies sites and a link to the Canadian Literature Archive. There is also a Canadian resource page, one on the Globe Theatre, and others on Canadian Universities' English Departments.

"The Most Frequently Banned Books in the 1990's." The top fifty banned books are listed. Some titles are surprising. (http://www.cs.cmu.edu/People/spok/most-banned.html)

Yahoo!—Arts: Humanities: Literature (http://www.yahoo.com/art/literature/) is one of the most comprehensive and useful literature sites on the Net. Authors, Awards, Bestseller Lists, Electronic Literature, Exhibits, Genres, Journals, Literary HyperCalendar, Magazines, Organizations, Reviews, and Scripts are some of the areas found here.

The Hall of Language and Literature (http://www.tenet.edu/academia/lang.html) contains many resources for K–12 educators and students. Areas include literature, journalism, and composition.

Electronic Resources for Youth Services (http://www.ccn.cs.dal.ca/~aa331/childlit.html) is dedicated to reviewing WWW resources related to children's literature and youth services. Contents include Award Winning Books, Book Reviews, Writing Resources, Educational Entertainment, and Online Children's Literature.

Research

The Library of Congress catalogs, library services, and research tools are helpful for researching various topics for the English classroom. (http://www.loc.gov)

AskERIC (http://webcrawler.com/select/ed.02.html) is a diverse online resource for teachers, administrators, and others in the field of education. Another address for AskERIC is http://ericir.syr.edu/

Young Adult Librarian's Help/Homepage (http://www.kcpl.lib.mo.us/ya/) lists sites appropriate for young adults. Sections here include Starting Points (young adult literature), Reading Pages (specific authors), Teen Pages (including magazines and other interesting sites for teens), and Ending Points (of particular interest to librarians). Lists of Best Books for Young Adults, Quick Picks for the Reluctant Young Reader, and Selected Films and Videos for Young Adults are available from this site.

Words

The Logical World of Etymology (http://www.phoenix.net/~melanie/thelogic.htm) provides information on a variety of topics about words. Word origins, Latin and Greek prefixes and roots, and etymology archives are some of the interesting aspects of this site. Questions regarding a specific word's origin and history are also answered here.

Writing

Researchpaper.com provides information about writing the research paper. A writing center, discussion area, idea directory, and chat room are there to help with the research paper. (http://www.researchpaper.com/)

Purdue OWL: Writing Resources (http://owl.english.purdue.edu/writing.html) contains a variety of resources to help in the writing process. Reference resources, guides to style and editing, indexes for writers, search tools and directories, and a terrific collection of over 100 handouts on writing skills are all here.

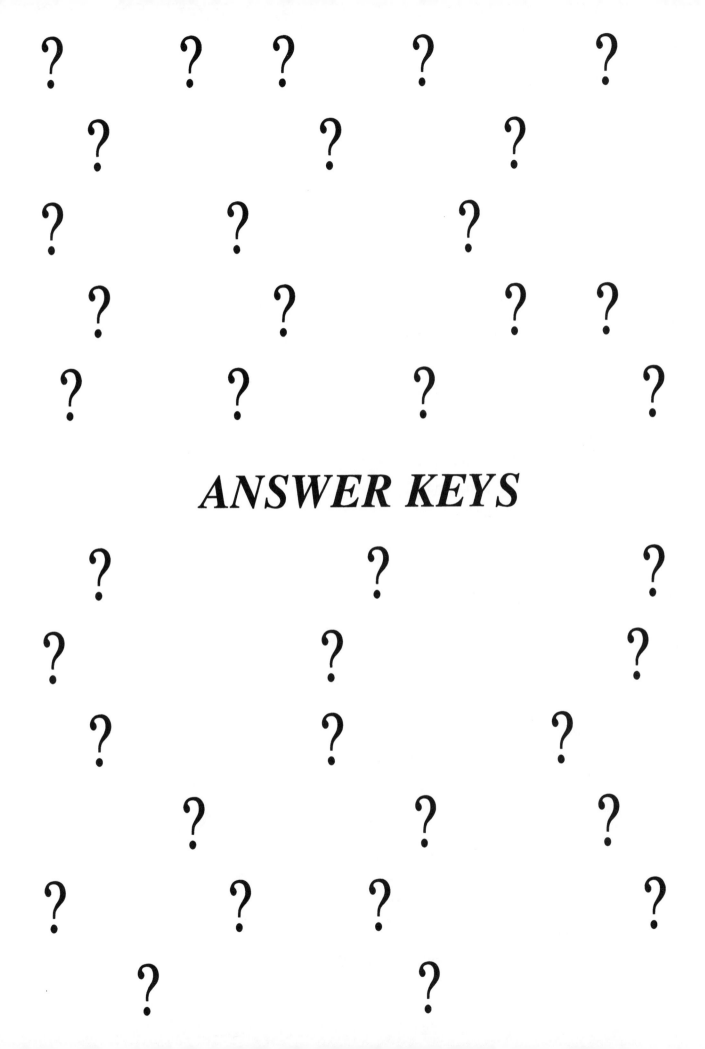

ANSWER KEYS

1. AND THE PART OF SPEECH IS...

1. adverb
2. preposition
3. adjective
4. verb
5. conjunction
6. preposition

7. interjection
8. noun
9. verb
10. conjunction
11. noun
12. preposition

2. FUN WITH PARTS OF SPEECH

1. adjective
2. verb
3. preposition
4. adverb
5. noun
6. noun
7. verb
8. verb
9. adjective
10. noun

11. adverb
12. noun
13. adjective
14. preposition
15. preposition
16. noun
17. noun
18. verb
19. noun
20. verb

3. SPREADING THE WEALTH

1. None (p), is (v), to (prep)
2. immediately (advb), and (c), project (n)
3. needy (adj), who (p)
4. Ugh (i), demands (v)
5. or (c)
6. gracefully (advb), crowded (adj), because (c), people (n)
7. Wow (i)
8. gloves (n), at (prep)
9. us (p), now (advb)
10. Ouch (i), walked (v), into (prep), cement (adj)

4. COMMON NOUNS ARE WHAT WE WANT!

1. necklace, overcoat
2. magician, announcement, news
3. implications, solutions
4. army, nonsense, inhabitants
5. specialist, laws, alimony, negotiations
6. dentist, enthusiasm, naming, teams
7. Indecisiveness, reality
8. eulogist, listeners, yelling
9. opportunity, furniture, inducement
10. teacher, students, economy
11. love, friends

The John Donne quotation is: "No man is an island entirely of itself."

5. IS THOMAS EDISON A PROPER OR A COMMON ONE?

1. l		14. j	
2. r		15. b	
3. s		16. g	
4. c		17. q	
5. o		18. x	
6. d		19. p	
7. w		20. i	
8. f		21. k	
9. v		22. e	
10. t		23. y	
11. u		24. h	
12. n		25. m	
13. a			

The three types of fish are cod (#'s 4-5-6), tuna (#'s 10-11-12-13), and pike (#'s 19-20-21-22).

6. A NOUN AND ITS USES

1. p.n.	4. s.	7. o.p.	10. app.	13. i.o.	16. o.p.
2. o.	5. o.	8. p.n.	11. o.p.	14. o.	17. s.
3. i.o.	6. app.	9. s.	12. i.o.	15. app.	18. p.n.

7. NINES ARE EVERYWHERE

1. All, them, me
2. One, us, them
3. He, she, some
4. Those, many
5. Nobody, her
6. Each, many, I
7. This, yours
8. Who, any, him
9. who, some, us
10. Anybody, it
11. you, they, me
12. ourselves
13. What, I, them
14. me, himself
15. I, much, that

8. THESE INDEFINITE PRONOUNS ARE DEFINITELY HIDDEN

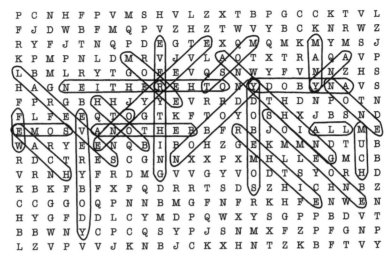

ALL	EITHER	MOST	SEVERAL
ANOTHER	EVERYBODY	MUCH	SOME
ANY	EVERYONE	NEITHER	SOMEBODY
ANYBODY	EVERYTHING	NOBODY	SOMEONE
ANYTHING	FEW	NONE	
BOTH	MANY	ONE	
EACH	MORE	OTHER	

9. FINDING FIVE VERBS

The prepositional phrases are:

1. By Thursday, on the plane, over Los Angeles
2. to the complaints, during the raucous meeting
3. of students, without lunch passes
4. Near my locker, before lunch, about the problems, in Bosnia
5. toward the horizon
6. like his brother
7. on the bandwagon
8. around the set, during the rehearsals
9. near the taxi station
10. Around the league
11. inside his pocket, like this

The verbs spelled out are: boot, down, bait, load, and nail.

10. ONLY CERTAIN LETTERS COUNT HERE!

The verbs are:

Group A

1. schemed
2. gathering
3. weaving
4. owns
5. innovate

The famous person and place is <u>Washington</u>.

Group B

6. identified
7. provided
8. overcome
9. celebrate
10. enjoyed

The famous American city is <u>Providence</u> (Rhode Island).

11. LOOKING FOR THOSE ADJECTIVES

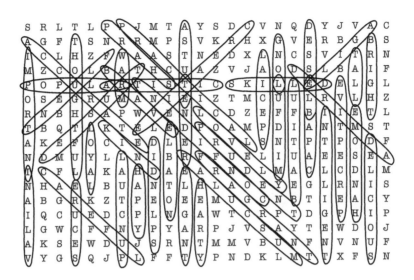

ACCURATE	CREATIVE	LOVELY	SKILLED
ADMIRED	DELICIOUS	LOYAL	SPECIAL
AGILE	ELEGANT	MINDFUL	SPLENDID
ARTISTIC	FLUENT	MUSCULAR	TALL
ASTUTE	FRAGRANT	NOTABLE	TENDER
BEAUTIFUL	HANDSOME	PERCEPTIVE	THOUGHTFUL
BLESSED	HAPPY	POPULAR	TRUSTED
BRAVE	HEARTY	PRACTICAL	VALIANT
BRIGHT	IMPORTANT	PRUDENT	WARM
CAPABLE	INTELLIGENT	PUNCTUAL	
CAREFUL	KIND	SECURE	
CONFIDENT	LONG	SHARP	

12. ANIMALS AND ADVERBS

1. gladly
2. Evidently, often
3. recently, newly
4. not, immediately, exceedingly
5. there, slowly, hopefully
6. Later, kindly
7. more, rapidly
8. only
9. too, early, completely
10. intelligently, accurately
11. openly
12. youthfully

The five animals are: the tiger, lion, monkey, cat, and horse.

13. PREPOSITIONS AND DRINKS

The prepositions are:

1. through, except
2. across
3. concerning, over
4. like, at
5. Since, over, during, at
6. Within, into
7. near, except
8. to, of, near
9. in, concerning,
10. Within, across, toward
11. except
12. regarding

The six drinks are: tea, cola, soda, wine, tonic, and water.

14. OVER THE RIVER AND THROUGH THE WOODS TO GRANDMOTHER'S HOUSE WE GO

1. without exercise
2. except Sundays
3. Since 1995
4. toward his goal
5. past his original goal
6. Over the summer
7. in the long race
8. near Toronto, Canada
9. Throughout the spring
10. from his workout routine
11. Like his older sister
12. under any weather conditions
13. In many circumstances
14. during his training
15. About three weeks ago
16. by himself
17. concerning his fitness

The famous place along the Hudson River in New York is *West Point.*

Something our body needs is *fluid.*

The famous trio of letters is *a-b-c.*

15. THE TWENTY-FIVE PREPOSITIONAL PHRASES

1. in the morning, to school
2. Without our approval, on Tuesday night, at ten o'clock
3. Over the river, through the woods, to grandmother's house
4. (none)
5. (none)
6. near the door, beyond the tables
7. of the bread, in the city, on the counter
8. under the couch, by the bureau
9. to the first baseman
10. in the elementary school orchestra, without their director, for a quarter, of an hour
11. between Tricia and me
12. past your room, at the cat
13. (none)
14. (none)
15. by your uncle, for two hundred dollars

16. FANBOY AND W.N. BEN

The following are the conjunctions in the sentences:

1. and
2. Either...or
3. but
4. or
5. for
6. not only...but also
7. both...and
8. Neither...nor
9. but
10. whether...or
11. nor

17. SUBORDINATING CONJUNCTIONS

1. WHETHER	6. THOUGH	11. BEFORE	16. LEST
2. AFTER	7. WHENEVER	12. WHEN	17. THAT
3. BECAUSE	8. WHERE	13. UNLESS	18. UNTIL
4. SINCE	9. AS	14. THAN	19. WHEREVER
5. ALTHOUGH	10. WHATEVER	15. IF	20. WHILE

18. SIMPLE SUBJECTS AND THE HIDDEN SENTENCE

1. thermometers	7. Natives
2. issue	8. sky
3. timidity	9. They
4. Measurements	10. embarrassment
5. We	11. Anyone
6. carpet	

The hidden sentence is: This time we can ask the man.

19. CONSTRUCTING SENTENCES

Possible sentences are as follows.

1. She walked into the room.
2. Jill will clean the car.
3. Juan and he walked slowly.
4. Will you help her?
5. He and Tim should see them.
6. We carefully hid the gifts.
7. Carefully lock the door.
8. Could they join us at noon?
9. The boys had started the game eagerly.
10. Paint it during class.

20. FILL AND COMPLETE

1. noun	6. preposition
2. verb	7. conjunction
3. pronoun/noun	8. verb
4. adverb	9. verb
5. adjective	10. interjection

21. SAME WORD. . .DIFFERENT PARTS OF SPEECH

1. noun	6. preposition	11. preposition
2. adjective	7. adverb	12. conjunction
3. verb	8. adjective	13. noun
4. noun	9. preposition	14. noun
5. verb	10. adverb	15. verb

22. DOUBLE-DUTY WORDS

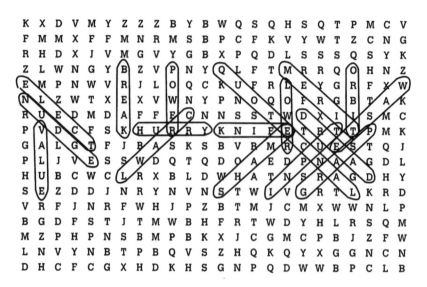

BREAK	HURRY	NUDGE	VALUE
CRAWL	INPUT	ORBIT	WASTE
DREAD	KNIFE	POWER	
ELECT	LANCE (OR LOWER)	QUOTE	
GRASP	MERIT	SHAME	

23. WIN, PLACE, AND SHOW

1. bid (2) noun and verb

2. down (3) adjective, adverb, noun, preposition, and verb,

3. into (1) preposition

4. key (3) adjective, noun, and verb

5. major (3) adjective, noun, and verb

6. pick (2) noun and verb

7. retail (3) adjective, adverb, noun, and verb

8. severe (1) adjective

9. snow (3) adjective, noun, and verb

10. token (3) adjective, noun, and verb

The six winners are the words down, key, major, retail, snow, and token. Second place finishers are bid and pick. Third place finishers are into and severe.

24. PARTS OF SPEECH MAGIC SQUARE

A = 15	B = 6	C = 9	D = 4
E = 12	F = 1	G = 14	H = 7
I = 2	J = 11	K = 8	L = 13
M = 5	N = 16	O = 3	P = 10

25. GRAMMAR REVIEW

1. (He) knew the correct answer to the difficult problem.
2. The (magician) cleverly performed the trick during the show.
3. Throughout my childhood, (I) played the guitar and the piano.
4. (This) is not a story about a new movie.
5. (We) wheeled the patient past the crowded room.
6. My (mother) had smelled smoke in the kitchen.
7. (It) is written with his trademark style.
8. The (play) is a comedy written by a famous playwright.
9. (All) of the money was found near the desk.
10. (I) definitely received very little information from him.

26. WILL THE REAL GERALD R. FORD PLEASE STAND UP?

1. (L) Sly
2. (E) had
3. (S) Sly
4. (L) to help
5. (I) his
6. (E) verb
7. (L) friend's
8. (Y) he
9. (N) finished

10. (C) for camp
11. (H) project
12. (K) When
13. (I) he
14. (N) past
15. (G) a fragment followed by a complete sentence
16. (J) his
17. (R) to and for

President Gerald R. Ford was born *Leslie Lynch King, Jr.* in 1913. When Ford's mother remarried, he was given the name Gerald R. Ford.

(Source: *The Book of Answers*, p. 247)

27. GRAMMAR AND USAGE CROSSWORD

28. FINAL TEST ON CONJUNCTIONS AND PREPOSITIONS

Conjunctions

1. until
2. Both...and
3. Before, and
4. Not only... but also
5. When, for
6. As, and
7. Because

Prepositional Phrases

1. on Mount Draper, in the morning
2. After the last time
3. throughout the day
4. to Florida, during the winter recess
5. before breakfast, of the day
6. above ninety degrees
7. on the beach

29. FINAL TEST ON PARTS OF SPEECH

1. noun
2. verb
3. preposition
4. adverb
5. adjective
6. pronoun
7. conjunction
8. preposition
9. pronoun
10. noun
11. interjection
12. adjective
13. pronoun
14. preposition
15. pronoun
16. verb
17. adverb
18. noun
19. adjective
20. verb

30. FINAL TEST ON PHRASES AND CLAUSES

1. (D) noun clause
2. (G) adverb phrase
3. (B) adjective clause
4. (A) independent clause
5. (B) adjective clause
6. (A) independent clause
7. (I) infinitive phrase
8. (J) gerund phrase
9. (E) verb phrase
10. (D) noun clause
11. (G) adverb phrase
12. (A) independent clause
13. (F) adjective phrase
14. (H) participial phrase
15. (J) gerund phrase
16. (F) adjective phrase
17. (H) participial phrase
18. (I) infinitive phrase
19. (C) adverb clause
20. (C) adverb clause

31. DID I DO GOOD OR DID I DO WELL???

A. affect   F. fewer   K. than

B. Besides   G. well   L. effect

C. among   H. teach   M. Take

D. Bring   I. Leave   N. as

E. discover   J. like   O. among

The winning team is *Team B* with 15 points. *Team A* has 7 points.

32. DID THE DOE EAT THE DOUGH?

A = 11	B = 13	C = 8	D = 2
E = 4	F = 6	G = 15	H = 9
I = 5	J = 3	K = 10	L = 16
M = 14	N = 12	O = 1	P = 7

The homophones of the words in the puzzle are below.

A. beer   E. intense   I. least   M. grown

B. stare   F. flour   J. waist   N. bread

C. are   G. rest   K. higher   O. doe

D. oral   H. miner   L. symbol   P. choose

33. WHOM DO YOU TRUST?

1. D   5. M   9. O   13. N

2. H   6. A   10. B   14. C

3. J   7. K   11. I   15. P

4. G   8. E   12. F   16. L

34. A MAGIC SQUARE FEATURING WORDS THAT ARE OFTEN CONFUSED

A = 13	B = 3	C = 6	D = 12
E = 8	F = 10	G = 15	H = 1
I = 11	J = 5	K = 4	L = 14
M = 2	N = 16	O = 9	P = 7

35. DOES THIS STORY HAVE A MORALE?

1. adapt
2. affect
3. bazaar
4. proceeded
5. indignant
6. incredulous
7. lest
8. quiet
9. physical
10. Altogether
11. distracted
12. dispersed
13. corporation
14. commend
15. area
16. annual
17. difference
18. their
19. extent
20. emerging

36. WRITE THE RIGHT WORDS

1. seller, cellar
2. bare, bear
3. tale, tail
4. None, nun
5. our, hour
6. maid, made
7. knew, new
8. raise, raze
9. lie, lye
10. sale, sail
11. heel, heal
12. guessed, guest
13. not, knot
14. hear, here
15. seem, seam

37. IRREGULAR VERBS

1. CHOSEN	11. FLOWN
2. DRUNK	12. GIVEN
3. BEGUN	13. WRITTEN
4. BROUGHT	14. RUNG
5. THROWN	15. SWUM
6. DRIVE	16. DRAWN
7. SUNG	17. SAID
8. BITTEN	18. STOLEN
9. COME	19. DONE
10. EATEN	20. FALLEN

38. MORE IRREGULAR VERBS

1. KNOWN	11. RIDDEN
2. LOST	12. FLUNG
3. GOTTEN	13. BEATEN
4. LED	14. CAUGHT
5. LENT	15. FROZEN
6. SHAKEN	16. STUNG
7. BROKEN	17. CREPT
8. GONE	18. RUN
9. GROWN	19. BURST
10. SEEN	20. BORNE

Letter Substitution Code Used:

Letter: A B C D E F G H I J K L M N O P Q R S T U V W X Y Z

Code: M U N L W R C T S X Z J F H E B D Q V K I Y O A P G

39. IRREGULAR VERBS AND THREE COUNTRIES

1. dealt	10. caught
2. spun	11. drank
3. stung	12. slid
4. sprang	13. spoke
5. spat	14. swum
6. rung	15. worn
7. wept	16. torn
8. swam	17. slept
9. drawn	18. gotten

The three countries the letters form are Panama, Peru, and Portugal.

40. HOW MANY N'S ARE THERE?

1. drove	8. beaten
2. sung	9. hidden
3. wept	10. spun
4. woven	11. swept
5. shaken	12. burst
6. hanged	13. leaped
7. borne	

The letter n appears 5 times.

41. ACTIVE AND PASSIVE VOICES

1. passive	9. passive
2. active	10. passive
3. passive	11. active
4. passive	12. active
5. active	13. active
6. passive	14. active
7. active	15. passive
8. passive	

The Active Voice had 15 points and the Passive Voice had 16 points. The winner is the Passive Voice!

42. POSITIVE...COMPARATIVE...SUPERLATIVE...

1. happier	9. more (or less) often
2. more (or most) recent	10. better
3. most (or least) beautiful	11. more (or less) favorably
4. youngest	12. prettier
5. more (or most) useful	13. sooner
6. simplest	14. more
7. worse	15. rougher
8. most (or least) practical	

43. MODIFYING THE MODIFIERS

Here are some possible answers:

2. While I (he, she, Jerry, etc.) was cleaning the bathroom, the phone rang.

3. The boys in our van saw the magician performing his tricks.

4. Marcia detected an unpleasant smell inside the freezer.

5. From the window we watched him score the basket.

6. I heard the noise inside the car's engine.

7. Dad spotted the neighbor's cat eating our cat's food.

8. We sell shoes with rubber soles to senior high school students.

9. Looking through her telescope, the scientist saw the moon.

10. The bulb in the flashlight was fixed by the man.

11. The hostess served the steak on her finest plates to the guests.

12. While they were walking to school, the children spotted the bus.

44. DOUBLE NEGATIVES

The sentences that have the double negative problem are: 1, 3, 6, 8, 11, and 12. The word that can be placed in front of parachute, calf, and cow is <u>golden</u>.

45. CAPITAL LETTERS

1. Arizona, Boston
2. Congressman, David
3. Eagerly, French
4. Grand, Hoover
5. Indian
6. Justifying, Kentucky
7. Lithuanian, Mr.
8. Nearly, Omaha
9. Prom
10. Q., Revolution
11. Station, Towers
12. Until
13. Violent
14. Walkman
15. Xerxes, Yalta
16. Zachary

The words that need to be capitalized are in alphabetical order.

46. AN ABBREVIATED JOURNEY

Je = June   mi. = miles   DC = District of Columbia
A.D. = Anno Domini   Rev. = Reverend   Mem. = Memorial
Dr. = Doctor   Robt. = Robert   Penn. = Pennsylvania
Mrs. = Mistress   Bros. = Brothers   Ave. = Avenue
Sr. = Senior   Inc. = Incorporated   bldg. = building
NY = New York   Capt. = Captain   Riv. = River
NJ = New Jersey   Prof. = Professor   htl. = hotel
secs. = seconds   rest. = restaurant   sens. = senators
Rd. = Road   mos. = months   nxt. = next
tpke. = turnpike   pct. = percent   yr. = year
degs. = degrees   m.p.h. = miles per hour
km. = kilometers   Wash. = Washington

47. PERFECTING PUNCTUATION

1. comma   11. semicolon   21. comma
2. period   12. period   22. period
3. exclamation point   13. colon   23. comma
4. period   14. comma   24. period
5. period   15. period   25. parentheses
6. quotation marks   16. dash   26. parentheses
7. question mark   17. dash   27. period
8. quotation marks   18. period   28. period
9. period   19. period   29. period
10. period   20. comma   30. period

48. SOMETHING'S UP WITH SIXTY-SEVEN

1. Change *ain't no* to *isn't any* or *is no*
2. Change *he* to *him*
3. C
4. Omit *most*
5. C
6. Change *due* to *do.*
7. C
8. C
9. C
10. C
11. C
12. Change *carry* to *carries.*
13. Change *libary* to *library.*
14. C
15. Change *massage* to *message.*

49. I CAN'T GET NOTHING RIGHT TODAY!

1. Change *accept* to *except.*
2. Change *less* to *fewer.*
3. Change *hisself* to *himself.*
4. Change *respectively* to *respectfully.*
5. Change *swam* to *swum.*
6. Change *amount* to *number.*
7. Change *soft* to *softly.*
8. Change *good* to *well.*
9. Change *busted* to *broken.*
10. Change *between* to *among.*
11. Change *him* to *he.*
12. Change *where* to *that.*
13. Change *was* to *were.*
14. Change *have* to *has.*
15. Change *of* to *have.*

50. USAGE CROSSWORD PUZZLE

51. USAGE PRETEST

1. fragment
2. complete sentence
3. fragment
4. run-on
5. is
6. were
7. were
8. is
9. are
10. Have
11. her
12. them
13. whom
14. who
15. himself
16. she
17. your
18. torn
19. sprung
20. rising
21. have
22. happy
23. terrible
24. most
25. have

52. FINAL TEST ON USAGE

1. complete sentence
2. fragment
3. complete sentence
4. run-on
5. is
6. Have
7. was
8. seems
9. Doesn't
10. are
11. is
12. is
13. was
14. doesn't
15. are
16. were
17. I
18. her
19. whom
20. whom
21. I
22. driven
23. were
24. well
25. take

53. IS IT OCTOPUSES OR OCTOPI?

1. children
2. churches
3. bases
4. salmon
5. cupfuls
6. Smiths
7. women
8. criteria
9. brothers-in-law
10. tomatoes
11. embryos
12. leaves
13. passersby
14. summaries
15. boxes
16. media
17. beaux
18. oases
19. donkeys
20. indices
21. lives
22. vetoes
23. 7's
24. radios
25. t's

54. MAKING THEM ALL AGREE!

Group 1	Group 2	Group 3
1. is (1)	1. seem (2)	1. Was (1)
2. are (2)	2. has (2)	2. are (1)
3. was (3)	3. is (1)	3. have (2)
4. need (1)	4. believes (3)	4. Does (3)
5. knows (2)	5. are (1)	5. require (2)

55. FINAL TEST ON AGREEMENT

1. was	5. didn't	9. is	13. were	17. was
2. is	6. was	10. have	14. Are	18. is
3. is	7. has	11. are	15. is	19. makes
4. were	8. are	12. were	16. are	20. needs

56. KNOWING THOSE ROOTS AND PREFIXES

1. isla	9. ntis
2. mjud	10. mrom
3. aism	11. anca
4. shin	12. thol
5. tota	13. icwo
6. oism	14. rldr
7. prot	15. elig
8. esta	16. ions

The letters spell out the following: Islam, Judaism, Shinto, Taoism, Protestantism, Roman Catholic, World Religions

57. PREFIXES AND BASES

1. G	5. B	9. F	13. K
2. D	6. J	10. P	14. C
3. A	7. E	11. M	15. H
4. L	8. O	12. N	16. I

58. PREFIXES CROSSWORD

59. ROOTS AND PREFIXES

1. G	6. E	11. K	16. R
2. D	7. L	12. B	17. O
3. J	8. S	13. C	18. F
4. H	9. P	14. M	19. N
5. A	10. I	15. Q	20. T

60. LATIN AND GREEK STEMS

1. sing	14. thermo
2. tooth	15. inscribe
3. order	16. logy
4. rule	17. loq
5. eu	18. manu
6. sound	19. inspect
7. agr	20. death
8. rupt	21. naut
9. earth	22. incur
10. one	23. greg
11. pater	24. hydr
12. end	25. touch
13. name	

The words that eager shoppers love to hear are "Stores are open till midnight."

61. SIX COMMON TYPES OF ANALOGIES

1. d	10. b
2. c	11. a
3. f	12. e
4. f	13. c
5. a	14. d
6. f	15. e
7. d	16. a
8. b	17. e
9. b	18. c

62. ANALYZING ANALOGIES

a. 12   g. 9

b. 3   h. 5

c. 10   i. 4

d. 1   j. 7

e. 11   k. 6

f. 2   l. 8

63. AN ANALOGY CROSSWORD PUZZLE

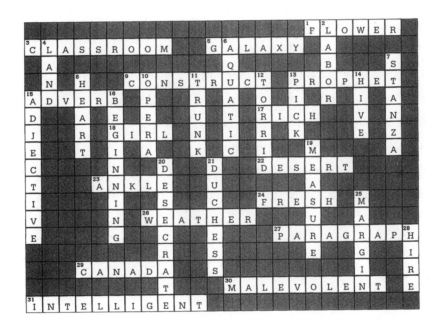

64. MAKING UP YOUR OWN ANALOGIES

Possible answers include the following analogies.

2. set: place   Set is a synonym for place. Both are verbs.

3. set: group   A set is a group, for example, in square dancing.

4. school: fish   A group of fish is called a school.

5. school: learn   A school is where one will learn.

6. strip: clothes   To strip is to remove the clothes.

7. strip: land   A strip is a piece of land.

8. level : tool   A level is a type of tool.

9. level: even   If something is level, it is even.

10. cast: play   A cast is the group of actors in a play.

11. cast: hurl   To cast an object is to hurl it. They are synonyms.

12. charge: responsibility   A charge is one's responsibility.

13. charge: purchase   One may charge (bill) a purchase.

14. cross: angry   If one is cross, he is angry.

15. cross: road   One may cross (or go over) a road.

16. square: mathematics   A square is a term used in mathematics.

17. square: equalize   To square something is to equalize it.

18. seal : water   A seal is a water carnivore.

19. seal : envelope   To secure an envelope, you seal it.

20. seal: genuine   A seal indicates that the document bearing the seal is genuine.

65. ADJECTIVES FROM A TO Z

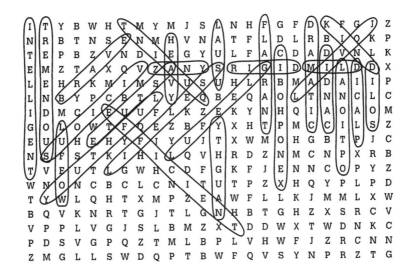

ASTUTE	HEAVY	OPTIONAL	VICIOUS
BRAVE	INTELLIGENT	PLACID	WOEFUL
CANDID	JOVIAL	QUAINT	XENOPHOBIC
DRAMATIC	KIND	RIGID	YOUTHFUL
EFFICIENT	LIFELESS	SOLID	ZANY
FLAGRANT	MILD	TREMENDOUS	
GLEEFUL	NAUGHTY	USUAL	

66. VOCABULARY AND ADJECTIVES

Though answers will vary for these words, the x word space was created with the word xenophobic in mind.

67. SELECTING THE RIGHT WORD FOR THE RIGHT PERSON

1. witty
2. articulate
3. punctual
4. honest
5. unpretentious
6. inquisitive
7. devoted
8. empathetic
9. motivated
10. creative
11. scholarly
12. expressive
13. diligent
14. stable
15. indomitable

68. IS IT AS SIMPLE AS A, B, C, OR D?

1. B	6. B	11. D	16. D
2. A	7. A	12. B	17. B
3. B	8. A	13. D	18. D
4. B	9. C	14. D	19. A
5. A	10. A	15. D	20. D

A. 6   B. 6   C. 1   D. 7

D is the winning letter with seven answers.

69. HOW MANY DIFFERENT WAYS CAN IT BE DONE?

1. c	6. e	11. j
2. h	7. m	12. o
3. a	8. i	13. b
4. n	9. l	14. f
5. g	10. k	15. d

The three words found in the answer key are change (1–6), milk (7–10) and job (11–13).

70. READING PEOPLE'S MOODS

Though answers will vary, these are possible answers.

2. boredom, tiredness

3. scorn, contempt

4. complacency, conceit

5. silliness

6. amusement

7. pain, contempt, disgust

8. sorrow, relief, fatigue, longing

9. malicious triumph

10. worry, boredom

11. thoughtfulness, boredom

12. amusement, mild disbelief

13. boredom, fatigue

14. anger, disappointment

15. embarrassment, sadness, dejection

71. WHEN IS A SMILE A GRIN? WHEN IS A LAUGH A GUFFAW?

Possible answers may include the following words.

1. hurl, toss, fling

2. dart, dash, flee, abscond, operate, govern

3. injure, harm, wrong, impair, maim, cripple

4. heartless, sunless, chilled, numbed, unconscious, passionless, unfriendly, unsociable

5. battle, combat, duel, assault, attack, warfare

6. virtuous, moral, righteous, honorable

7. hefty, weighty, bulky, substantial, dense

8. large, enormous, huge, massive, colossal, immense

9. obvious, simple, plain, effortless, lenient

10. interrogate, question, appeal, demand, quiz

11. wicked, evil, sinister, defective, faulty, tainted, spoiled, virtueless, corrupt

12. touch, probe, grope, sense, caress, perceive, note

13. perceive, discern, observe, understand, know, comprehend,

14. agreeable, pleasant, gratifying, pleasing, delightful, attractive, likable

15. enjoy, prize, esteem, appreciate, savor

72. WHY IS A SANDAL BETTER THAN THE OTHER TWO?

Here are some possible answers.

1.	furniture	chair	captain's chair
2.	vehicle	car	station wagon
3.	literature	novel	romance novel
4.	science	chemistry	organic chemistry
5.	road	highway	Highway 61
6.	sport	contact sport	football
7.	animal	dog	cocker spaniel
8.	food	vegetable	carrot
9.	music	rock	hard rock
10.	group	team	cheerleaders
11.	musical instrument	guitar	bass guitar
12.	game	board game	checkers
13.	merchandise	beverage	orange juice
14.	human being	woman	grandmother
15.	clothing	hat	baseball cap
16.	entertainment	movies	comedy movies
17.	machine	camera	video camera
18.	fruit	apple	green apple
19.	emotion	happiness	ecstasy
20.	tool	saw	chainsaw

73. ODD ONE OUT

1. (underpass) Underpass has nothing to do with ideas and beliefs. It's a path or road.
2. (negate) All the other words mean to go up or over.
3. (channel) Channel is not a weapon.
4. (ornery) The other words are ways to do things without definite direction.
5. (nimble) The others are ways to do things without definite purpose.
6. (veneer) The others mean to pay deep respect to.
7. (embroil) The others mean to go back or become less.
8. (negligence) The others have to do with when one is in control.
9. (trample) Trample does not mean to start.

10. (invade) The others mean to take something to a place.

11. (oust) The others mean to help.

12. (nonentity) The others are used for recording information.

13. (aspire) The others are antonyms of help.

14. (lag) the others mean to tempt.

The first letters of the fourteen correct answers spell UNCONVENTIONAL.

74. THE NAME GAME

1. ro	6. fr	11. rk	16. th	21. ia
2. be	7. an	12. ky	17. om	22. ha
3. rt	8. ci	13. le	18. as	23. nk
4. jo	9. ne	14. ka	19. sy	24. lo
5. hn	10. ma	15. ra	20. lv	25. ri
				26. bo

The names constructed by the answers are: Robert, John, Francine, Mark, Kyle, Kara, Thomas, Sylvia, Hank, Lori, and Bo. Thus, the Name Game is an appropriate title for this activity.

75. REVOLUTIONARY VOCABULARY

1. plu	6. eru	11. rcu	16. ssa
2. toe	7. ran	12. ryn	17. tur
3. art	8. usv	13. ept	18. n9p
4. hju	9. enu	14. une	19. lan
5. pit	10. sme	15. mar	20. ets

The revolutionaries are Pluto, Earth, Jupiter, Uranus, Venus, Mercury, Neptune, Mars, Saturn—9 planets. They all make revolutions around the sun!

76. ALL IN THE FAMILY

Possible answers include the following words.

Column A	Column B	Column C
1. deafness	deafening	deafen
2. annoyance	annoying	annoy
3. calmness	calm	calm
4. obsession	obsessive	obsess
5. expiration	expired	expire
6. derivation	derivative	derive
7. definition	definitive	define
8. narration	narrative	narrate
9. reformation	reformed	reform
10. repulsion	repulsive	repel
11. attraction	attractive	attract
12. enticement	enticing	entice
13. rebellion	rebellious	rebel
14. articulateness	articulate	articulate
15. commendation	commended	commend
16. acclamation	acclaimed	acclaim
17. instruction	instructive	instruct
18. prolongation	prolonged	prolong
19. restriction	restrictive	restrict
20. tyranny	tyrannical	tyrannize

77. HE HAD GROWN THE _____ PLANTS

1. laced

2. marker

3. glare

4. steam

5. teas

6. lament

7. blame

8. latent

9. teaser

10. room

11. stain

12. pesos

13. peaks

14. staple

15. sprite

78. STANDARD WORDS FOR STANDARDIZED TESTS

```
C R U I S E . . S P U R N . . . . . M A N I T O B A
O . . . T . . . . O . . F R E T . . . V . . . . . T
L . . . R . . C U R T A I L . . . . . . A B H O R . R
E . O . I . . A . O . . O . . . . . . . D . E . . . O
. B E N I G N . U . . . . B U S H . W O E . . . . . P
. S . . G . . . D . . . . . . T . A . O . . . . . . H
. R O M E . . . I . . . P . . R . N . T . . . . . . Y
. L . N . . . D A N . . L . V . B . D . . . . . . . .
. E . T . . . . . . . . I . E S O T E R I C . . . . J
. T . . . . . . . . . . A . R . R . R . G . . . . . O
P R E S L E Y . . . . . . B R A D . . . L . L I T H E
R . . W . . . . H . . . . L . C . . . A . O . . . . Y
. H A M . T O N G U E . . I . . . . . N . O . . . . U
F . M . . . C . . . . . . T . . . . . D . D . . . . .
A . . . . . K . . . . . . Y . . . . . . . E . . . . .
N . T H I R T E E N . . . . . . D A L M A T I A N S .
E . . . . . Y . . . . . . . . . . . . . . . U . . . .
```

79. FOUR-LETTER WORD SCRAMBLE

1. (p) aura	8. (l) site	15. (u) hone	22. (v) roam
2. (f) data	9. (e) sect	16. (a) sole	23. (o) plea
3. (m) oath	10. (j) heir	17. (k) heap	24. (h) gist
4. (b) beau	11. (q) dupe	18. (t) cite	25. (w) neon
5. (i) idle	12. (s) void	19. (d) élan	
6. (g) jest	13. (x) vain	20. (r) avow	
7. (n) idol	14. (y) yowl	21. (c) avid	

80. ONOMATOPOEIA—WORDS WITH SOME SMASH!

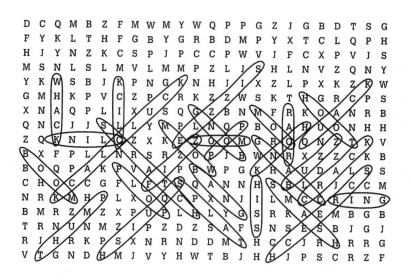

BANG	FIZZ	ROAR
BONG	HISS	SCRATCH
BOOM	HONK	SCREECH
BUZZ	HOOT	SIZZLE
CLACK	MEOW	SMASH
CLANG	MOO	SPLAT
CLICK	PLOP	SQUISH
CLINK	POP	THUMP
CLUCK	QUACK	WHACK
CRACK	RING	ZOOM

81. THE XYZ AFFAIR

```
X E R O X   Y A R D               Y
  M         E               X Y L E M
  A   Y   Y E S T E R D A Y     E   N
Y E S H I V A           O       A
A     E   K       Z     Y   X R A Y
  Y O L K         O   Z O N E     A
  A   D         Y O G A     N     C
  W             E     N     O     H
Z I N C   Z O D I A C   Y     N   T
I         E       R   Z
G         R   X E N O P H O B I A
Z I P   Z O O M       O
A       I       Y E L L O W
G       T       E     O
        H       A     G
      Y E W     S   Y U M M Y
        R       T
```

82. PUTTING THE PIECES TOGETHER

accurate	gruesome	sophomore
correlative	hybrid	suave
foreign	laboratory	tyranny
fraction	messenger	wholesome
gossamer	receive	wrestle

83. YOU *CAN* DO THIS!

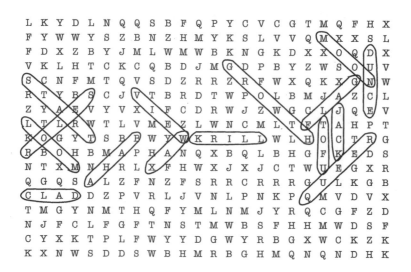

84. WHEN ONE LETTER FOLLOWS THE OTHER

Ahab = a famous captain

clad = dressed

dunce = a stupid person

flag = a piece of cloth

growth = the process of developing

jack = tool found in a trunk's car

krill = the main food of whalebone whales

loom = a machine for weaving thread

moon = a celestial body

queer = odd

roles = parts in a play

start = commence

tofu = a cheeselike food high in protein

view = sight or vision

wax = to increase

85. WHAT FOLLOWS WAR

86. DON'T BE FACETIOUS! IT'S TIME TO THINK ABOUT WORDS!

1. abstemious

2. Suggested words are physics, pneumonia, and psychology.

3. Suggested words are cloud, cub, and custom.

4. Suggested words are bough, though, through, and trough.

5. A suggested word is adamant.

6. Cemetery is a possible answer.

7. Illicit is a possible answer.

8. Bookworm is a possible answer.

9. A suggested word is usury.

10. Aardvark is a possible answer.

11. There are many possible answers. Eerie is one of them.

12. Skiing is a possible answer.

13. Brook is one of many answers.

14. Vacuum is a possible answer.

87. EUPHEMISMS

1. l	6. f	11. a
2. g	7. n	12. h
3. i	8. b	13. c
4. k	9. e	14. j
5. d	10. m	15. o

88. LEARNING FROM THE GRATE DEPRESSION

1. great	9. some
2. tale	10. None
3. weather	11. sons
4. There	12. mailed
5. fined	13. pieces
6. loan	14. maids
7. whole	15. past
8. read	

89. DUE DO DEW YOU YEW KNOW NO SOME SUM HOMOPHONES?

A = 1	B = 15	C = 8	D = 10
E = 4	F = 14	G = 5	H = 11
I = 13	J = 3	K = 12	L = 6
M = 16	N = 2	O = 9	P = 7

The homophones of the sixteen words are

air = oxygen

beer = drink

bread = food

chilly = cold

choose = elect

doe = female deer

flour = finely ground meal of wheat

grown = past participle of grow

higher = above

intense = extreme

least = smallest

miner = someone who works in a mine.

oral = relating to the mouth

rest = to recline; the remainder

symbol = representation

waist = middle part of the human body

90. TWO-WORD DEFINITIONS FOR THOSE CONFUSING HOMOPHONES

Column A	Column B
1. bear	1. beat
2. beech	2. sell
3. beet	3. die
4. beer	4. flee
5. blue	5. freeze
6. break	6. groan
7. cellar	7. hail
8. choir	8. heal
9. colonel	9. need
10. counsel	10. knot
11. fare	11. mail
12. flea	12. pain
13. flu	13. pause
14. flower	14. prey
15. pair	15. raise
16. plane	16. slay
17. principle	17. stare
18. reek	18. steal
19. tale	19. wade
20. two	20. wear

91. DOUBLE SIXES

1. all ready	9. heal
4. Take	11. metal
6. choose	12. past
8. farther	15. their

The total of these sentences is 66.

92. HAVE YOU EVER HAD DESSERT IN THE DESERT?

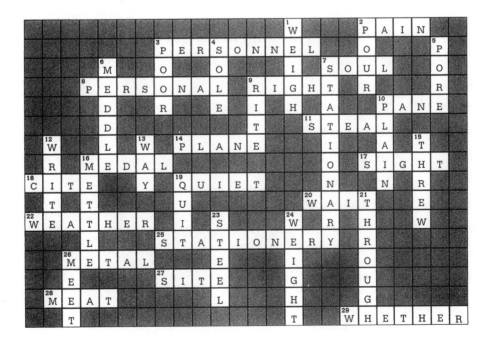

93. WORDS WE OFTEN CONFUSE

94. TAKING A COMPUTER APART

1. come	16. pore
2. compute	17. port
3. cope	18. pout
4. core	19. prom
5. court	20. rope
6. crop	21. rote
7. cruet	22. rout
8. crump	23. route
9. cute	24. term
10. cuter	25. tome
11. mope	26. tore
12. more	27. tour
13. mute	28. troupe
14. outer	29. truce
15. poet	30. trump

95. WHERE HAVE ALL THE LETTERS GONE?

1. dissatisfied	16. rhyme
2. occasionally	17. friend
3. mortgage	18. toward
4. courtesy	19. grammar
5. arrival	20. sophomore
6. annihilate	21. stubbornness
7. apparatus	22. written
8. blasphemy	23. aerial
9. mischief	24. connive
10. awfully	25. temperature
11. miniature	26. immature
12. addendum	27. analysis
13. changeable	28. relieve
14. penicillin	29. unnecessary
15. approval	30. succeed

The four famous names are Saturn, Philadelphia, Montana, and Maine.

96. HEADLINE READS "DID THE BELL OF THE BAWL DIE HER HARE?"

1. write...not...know
2. all...whether...whole...would...be
3. dear...raised...great...heard...their
4. their...week...heart...
5. Some...to...maid...
6. steak...for...pride...
7. vain...reigning...throne
8. sore... style...principal
9. vice
10. aisle...flowers...choir's...heard...by...guest
11. tale...son...due...time
12. birth
13. poor...we...see...meet
14. beat

97. LUCKY SEVEN...LUCKY THIRTEEN SPELLING

Section One

Group One: colossal (1)

Group Two: occurrence (1)

Group Three: gracious (4)

Group Four: reaction (3)

Group Five: utterance (2)

Group Six: twelfth (1)

Group Seven: seize (1)

Total: 13

Section Two

Group One: agile (3)

Group Two: deceit (2)

Group Three: stubborn (4)

Group Four: consistent (1)

Group Five: burial (1)

Group Six: dilemma (1)

Group Seven: nutrition (1)

Total: 13

98. MAKING THE SPELLING CONNECTION

1. S	6. K	11. Q	16. I
2. N	7. A	12. G	17. F
3. R	8. B	13. L	18. T
4. H	9. M	14. C	19. J
5. E	10. O	15. D	20. P

99. SPELLING EASE

1. absence	11. flagrant
2. mischief	12. forfeit
3. president	13. athletics
4. accident	14. general
5. specimen	15. privilege
6. medicine	16. correspond
7. souvenir	17. sulfur
8. argument	18. treasurer
9. enforcement	19. principal
10. exaggerate	20. illiterate

The connection between the introductory paragraph's first sentence and the answers is that each misspelled word involves the letter e. Either the letter e is omitted, is in the wrong place, or is inserted incorrectly in place of another letter. Thus, the pun on Spelling Ease involves all these e's. (Sorry!)

100. AN EVEN HUNDRED

The words that are spelled incorrectly are: (4) separate, (6) critical, (11) column, (12) burglar, (13) preferred, (16) success, (18) ignorance, and (20) believe. They total an even 100!

101. IS IT I BEFORE E OR E BEFORE I?

1. bel<u>ie</u>f
2. br<u>ie</u>f
3. spec<u>ie</u>s
4. anc<u>ie</u>nt
5. ach<u>ie</u>ve
6. h<u>ei</u>ght
7. sl<u>ei</u>gh
8. rec<u>ei</u>pt
9. th<u>ei</u>r
10. v<u>ei</u>l
11. dec<u>ei</u>t
12. for<u>ei</u>gn
13. l<u>ei</u>sure
14. r<u>ei</u>ns
15. n<u>ei</u>ther
16. rel<u>ie</u>ve
17. front<u>ie</u>r
18. pr<u>ie</u>st
19. f<u>ie</u>ld
20. consc<u>ie</u>nce

The words using the <u>ie</u> combination that add up to 105 are #'s 1, 2, 3, 4, 5, 16, 17, 18, 19, and 20. The remaining numbers use the <u>ei</u> combination and also add up to 105.

102. NICKELS AND DIMES, DOLLARS AND CENTS

1. picnic<u>k</u>ing
2. We<u>d</u>nesday
3. obs<u>c</u>ene
4. recom<u>m</u>end
5. paral<u>l</u>el
6. colum<u>n</u>
7. ad<u>d</u>ition
8. an<u>n</u>oy
9. ad<u>d</u>iction
10. Hawai<u>i</u>
11. incidental<u>l</u>y
12. ac<u>c</u>ustom
13. succe<u>e</u>d
14. at<u>t</u>endance
15. extraor<u>d</u>inary
16. bound<u>a</u>ry
17. an<u>n</u>ounce
18. se<u>e</u>the
19. inter<u>r</u>upt
20. practical<u>l</u>y
21. neces<u>s</u>ary
22. appro<u>a</u>ch
23. temper<u>a</u>ment
24. suppres<u>s</u>
25. occas<u>i</u>on
26. leisur<u>e</u>
27. un<u>n</u>ecessary
28. exces<u>s</u>ive
29. cons<u>c</u>ious
30. miscellane<u>o</u>us

103. FILLING IN THE MISSING LETTERS

Group 1
1. gracious (5)
2. peculiar (6)
3. conscious (5)
4. rhythm (5)
5. psychology (1)
Total points (22)

Group 2
1. discipline (4)
2. circuit (6)
3. sergeant (6)
4. doubtful (4)
5. remember (5)
Total points (25)

Group 3
1. Wednesday (3)
2. medieval (4)
3. February (4)
4. probably (6)
5. vengeance (6)
Total points (23)

Group 4
1. seize (3)
2. arctic (3)
3. symphony (5)
4. maneuver (4)
5. subtle (3)
Total points (18)

104. FORMING PLURALS

1. beliefs
2. surf
3. Swiss
4. elves
5. scissors
6. feet
7. dice
8. children
9. moose
10. politics
11. mice
12. sheep
13. series
14. salmon
15. deer
16. oxen
17. corps
18. women
19. thieves
20. tornados

The words whose spellings remain the same in both the singular and plural forms are: 2, 3, 5, 9, 10, 12, 13, 14, 15, and 17. The total is 100.

105. COURTING PLURALS

1. b	9. r
2. a	10. l
3. r	11. a
4. r	12. w
5. i	13. y
6. s	14. e
7. t	15. r
8. e	

The British word is <u>barrister</u> and its American equivalent is <u>lawyer</u>.

106. ELIMINATING THE CONFUSION ABOUT POSSESSIVES AND APOSTROPHES

1. f	11. a	21. g	31. c
2. c	12. b	22. a	32. a
3. a	13. h	23. h	33. a
4. a	14. c	24. a	34. f
5. b	15. a	25. b	35. f
6. b	16. a	26. a	36. f
7. a	17. a	27. e	37. c
8. e	18. h	28. b	38. b
9. c	19. d	29. d	39. h
10. a	20. a	30. c	40. a

107. LOOK WHAT'S MISSING!

1. I have found the answer.
2. Can you remember her telephone number?
3. In the middle of the movie, we heard a scream.
4. Your coach, the man in the brown coat, is friendly.
5. Though my friend is loud, he is not obnoxious.
6. I distinctly heard him say, "You're the one we have chosen."
7. John was given a specialized CD player; it was his first one.
8. He arrived at 8:47 and left at 10:32.
9. Dottie is a hard-working, intelligent woman.
10. There are thiry-two pencils in the box.
11. Gary, aren't you going to the shop today?
12. Bob would like to attend the sports conference today; however, he has to go to work at the mall.
13. Ben has just won a ten-speed bike.
14. The score, 71-21, shows how strong the Stamford basketball team really is.
15. Wayne said, "I'll see you later," and walked away.

108. FORMING A SENTENCE WITH CAPITAL LETTERS

The words requiring capital letters are: Charles, Anthony, Reynolds, Princess, Eileen, Dubuque, Iowa, Each, Meyer's, In, South, America, North, America, Norman, Childress, Indiana, Elegant, Normally, Thursday, Last, August, The, In, North, Theodore, Edwina, Rawlings, Mr., Frank, Olsen, Residents, Shortly, English, Indians, Zoos, Everybody, The, Herbert, Ellison, Dave, Andrews, and Yes.

The sentence for today is: Carpe diem is an ancient Latin term for seize the day.

109. BRITISH OR AMERICAN?

1. A	11. B
2. B	12. A
3. B	13. B
4. A	14. B
5. B	15. B
6. B	16. A
7. A	17. B
8. B	18. A
9. A	19. A
10. A	20. A

The British scored 21 points and the Americans scored 18 points. The Brits are the winners!

110. THE PUNCTUATION PLACE

1. (e) dash	7. (i) parentheses
2. (m) semicolon	8. (l) quotation marks
3. (b) bracket	9. (d) comma
4. (f) ellipsis	10. (g) exclamation mark
5. (c) colon	11. (a) apostrophe
6. (h) hyphen	12. (j) period
	13. (k) question mark

The three words are small, prom, and core.

111. CHECKING ON THE 75% EFFECTIVE SENTENCE CHECKER

1. Remove gone and insert went.
2. Remove effected and insert affected.
3. Remove boys' and insert boys.
4. Remove them and insert their.
5. Remove amount and insert number.
6. Remove I and insert me.
7. Remove was and insert were.
8. Remove me and insert I.
9. Remove weather and insert whether.
10. Spell controversy this way.

112. GETTING THE SENTENCE STRAIGHT

Possible sentences are:

1. The black beret was left near <u>the</u> door.
2. Was the television <u>program</u> interesting?
3. Your <u>wallet</u> must have been very expensive.
4. Mike <u>seldom</u> goes to the supermarket located on Sunrise Highway.
5. Rita and I will take the <u>trophy</u> to Tom's house.
6. Which <u>of</u> the twins is taller?
7. Did you ever realize how <u>funny</u> Ronnie is?
8. The card game <u>is</u> over.
9. Let this <u>be</u> a lesson for you!
10. Bring <u>it</u> here.

113. SENTENCE DIRECTIVES

Possible answers include the following.

1. He saw the movie last night.
2. After the game they slowly left.
3. The tall woman walked the dog near the beautiful lake in town.
4. Carefully take the jewels with you.
5. The man ran quickly around the track.

114. COMBINING SENTENCES

2. The $1,200 exercise machine that the family has moved from the basement to the den now gets used more often.

3. During our Sunday walk along the beach today, the sun was out and there were only a few walkers at the beach.

4. John's friend, Bob, who attends Colgate University and wants to be a doctor, will go to medical school after graduation.

5. This summer we will fish, swim, and boat on Cape Cod, Massachusetts, where we have vacationed for the past six summers.

6. In Mr. Redmond's social studies class today, we will have a test including twenty short answers and one essay on the American Revolution.

7. When ten inches of snow fell today, my father, using the snow blower, removed the snow from our driveway in two hours.

8. Tickets for five dollars per person will be available at the door for those who plan to attend this Friday night's dance in the gym.

115. THE CORRECT ORDER OF THINGS

1. D   A   B   C
2. C   D   B   A
3. D   B   A   C
4. A   C   B   D
5. B   D   C   A

116. STRINGING SENTENCES TOGETHER

Possible answers are found below.

1. The Olympic swimmer broke the pool record.

2. The U.S. Postal Service issued a commemorative Elvis stamp.

3. The living room couch was purchased at the department store.

4. Galileo invented the telescope.

5. Snow covered much of the country.

6. Vancouver is a city in Canada.

7. The expensive ring was stolen from Bentley's Jewelers.

8. S.E. Hinton wrote *The Outsiders*.

9. A stray dog was found outside our school.

10. The traitor was executed by his enemies.

117. CAUSE AND EFFECT WITH SOME CLAUSES

1. o	6. c	11. f
2. l	7. b	12. a
3. h	8. j	13. g
4. n	9. i	14. d
5. e	10. m	15. k

118. MOVING ALONG WITH TRANSITIONAL WORDS

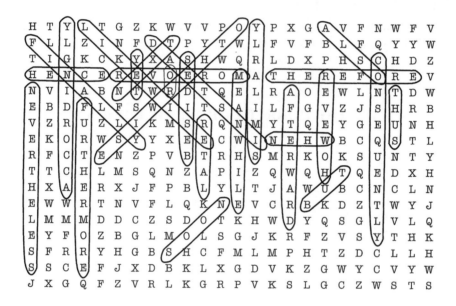

ACCORDINGLY	FURTHERMORE	MOREOVER	THEREFORE
AFTERWARD	HENCE	NEVERTHELESS	THUS
ALSO	HOWEVER	NEXT	WHEN
BESIDES	INSTEAD	OR	YET
BUT	LATER	OTHERWISE	
CONSEQUENTLY	LIKEWISE	SIMILARLY	
FINALLY	MEANWHILE	SOON	

119. TYING IDEAS TOGETHER

Answers will vary.

120. BRAINSTORMING...THE START OF THE WRITING PROCESS

Answers will vary.

121. BRAINSTORMING INTO A COMPOSITION

Answers will vary.

122. NOW THAT'S A GREAT IDEA!

Answers will vary.

123. MAKING THE ESSAY EASY (PART ONE)

1.	b	6.	t
2.	a	7.	h
3.	s	8.	o
4.	k	9.	l
5.	e	10.	d

The object is a <u>basket</u> (1–6) and its function is to <u>hold</u> (7–10).

124. MAKING THE ESSAY EASY (PART TWO)

1. iw
2. il
3. lg
4. et
5. an

6. Ao
7. nm
8. ye
9. ss
10. ay

"I will get an A on my essay."

125. SUPPORTING YOUR IDEAS

Answers will vary.

126. SOME FROM HERE AND SOME FROM THERE

Answers will vary.

127. CREATING A SCENE

Answers will vary.

128. CREATING DIALOGUE

Answers will vary.

129. A DAY IN THE LIFE

Answers will vary.

130. SEEING IT FROM ANOTHER'S EYES

Answers will vary.

131. USING YOUR WRITER'S TOOLBOX

Answers will vary.

132. DESCRIBING A PERSON

Answers will vary.

133. THE SPEECH'S PURPOSE

Answers will vary.

134. A CHECKLIST FOR CONSTRUCTING AN EFFECTIVE SPEECH

Answers will vary.

135. THE STYLE OF THE SPEECH

Answers will vary.

136. THE PURPOSE BEHIND THE OPENING LINE

Answers will vary.

137. LOOKING AT THE BEST

Answers will vary.

138. PREPARING A SPEECH

Answers will vary.

139. CHOOSING AND SUPPORTING ONE OVER THE OTHER

Answers will vary.

140. QUESTIONS ABOUT YOUR SPEECH

Answers will vary.

141. LITERARY TERMS CROSSWORD PUZZLE

```
                              1C      2H
                  3D I A L O G U E              5F    6M
          7C H A P T E R     U     N     M          I     O
   8B     H                A     T     F     O     9C     C     N
  10I M A G E R Y          M     O     L    11R E S O L U T I O N
   O     R                A     B     I     E     I     I     L
   G     A    13M              I     C     T     M     O     O
   R     C     O    14N        O     T     T     A     N     G
  15A U T H O R     N          G          I     X           U
   P     E     D   16N A R R A T O R      N        18N O V E L
   H     R          F     A     H         G
   Y                I     P     E    19S       20T
                    C     H    21M E T A P H O R
                    T     Y     E     A           N
                    I           N     E
                 22S Y M B O L        Z
                    N         23F L A S H B A C K
```

142. LITERARY TERMS CONSTRUCTION SITE

										C		H								
							D	I	A	L	O	G	U	E				F		M
		C	H	A	P	T	E	R		U		M						I		O
B		H					A		T		F		O			C		C		N
I	M	A	G	E	R	Y		M		O		L	R	E	S	O	L	U	T	I	O	N
O		R					A		B		I			E		I		L		
G		A	M			N			I		O			T		M		O		
R		C	O		N		O		T				T		A		N		
A	U	T	H	O	R		O	G				I		X			U		
P		E	D		N	A	R	R	A	T	O	R		N		N	O	V	E	L
H		R			F		A	H			G								
Y					I		P	E		S			T						
					C		H	M	E	T	A	P	H	O	R				
					T		Y	E		A			N						
					I			N		N			E						
		S	Y	M	B	O	L			Z									
					N			F	L	A	S	H	B	A	C	K			

143. SO MUCH TO READ, SO LITTLE TIME...

1. d	6. m	11. s	16. k
2. f	7. o	12. q	17. h
3. b	8. n	13. j	18. r
4. e	9. t	14. a	19. i
5. l	10. g	15. c	20. p

The famous race track is <u>Belmont</u> (3–9). The man's name is <u>Jack</u> (13–16). The synonym for tear is <u>rip</u> (18–20).

144. NEWSPAPER AND MAGAZINE TERMS

145. RECOGNIZING LITERARY SYMBOLS

```
W                 W  H  I  T  E        B
E  A  S  T        A           G  O  L  D              Y
S     P        W  A  T  E  R     A     R  O  S  E        F
T     R  E  D     K           E     C     I        L  I  O  N
      I     O  W  L           E     K  I  N  G     L     X
V     N     V     A  U  T  U  M  N        G        O
E  A  G  L  E     M     I                          W
N              B     G     S     F
U              H  E  R  C  U  L  E  S              T
S              P  R     A     A     E     F        H
               U     L     G     V     L           I
            B  R  I  D  G  E        E     I        R
               P        S           N  I  G  H  T
               L                    H        E
               E                    T        E
                                             N
```

146. WHAT DO YOU THINK THESE LITERARY QUOTATIONS MEAN?

Answers will vary.

147. LET'S GET STARTED

Answers will vary. Discussion is suggested.

148. A SHAKESPEAREAN SONNET

Answers may vary. These are possible answers.

1. sad...depressed...angered...pained

2. disgrace...alone...beweep...trouble deaf heaven...bootless cries...curse my fate

3. envious...jealous...unhappy

4. Wishing me like to one more rich in hope...Featur'd like him...Desiring this man's art, and that man's scope...With what I enjoy most contented least

5. happiness...joy...contentment

6. Haply I think on thee...my state sings hymns at heaven's gate...For thy love remembr'd such wealth brings...That then I scorn to change my state with kings

7. Yet

8. condition...life...situation

9. deaf heaven

10. The unhappy and alienated speaker curses his fate and cries out to an unconcerned heaven. Wanting to improve his life's condition, the speaker would like to have more hope, friends, and other talents and abilities. Though as saddened and envious as he does become, when he thinks of the love of another, he becomes elated and feels that he does not want to change his life because it is even better than the lives of kings.

149. ANALYZING A POEM

Answers will vary.

150. SOMETHING (OR NOTHING) IN COMMON

Answers will vary.

151. EXTENDING THE LIFE OF THE LITERARY CHARACTER

Answers will vary.

152. JUDGING A CHARACTER

Answers will vary.

153. NAMING YOUR CHARACTERS

Answers will vary.

154. THE NAMES OF LITERARY CHARACTERS

Answers will vary.

155. FAMOUS LITERARY CHARACTERS

```
                        ¹T  O  M  ²S  A  W  Y  E  ³R          ⁴R
    ⁵H  O  L  M  E  S              I      C      I              O
     Y              ⁶F  A  ⁷G  I  N          R  N          M        ⁸P
     D          ⁹B      I  U  K              O  N          E        O
 ¹⁰P ¹¹E  T  E  R  P  A  N      L      E          I  ¹²T  O  M      L
    I  I  O          N  L  R          G  E      U              L
    N  N  M              I  B          E  T  ¹³C  A  S  E  Y
    O  Y  B              V  E ¹⁴B      H  K              A
    C  T  O ¹⁵J ¹⁶A  N  E  L  A      E          ¹⁷R      N
    C  I  N      L  R  L  B          P              A  N
    H  M  E      I      ¹⁸W  A  T  S  O  N          P  A
    I      S      B          R          O              U
    O    ¹⁹D  R  A  C  U  L  A      ²⁰A  H  A  B      N
              B              L              Z
²¹B  L  A  C  K  B  E  A  U  T  Y      ²²C  I  N  D  E  R  E  L  L  A
                    C              C          L
          ²³F  R  A  N  K  E  N  S  T  E  I  N
```

156. SHAKING UP SHAKESPEARE

```
L O S T                               C R E S S I D A
E   H                       K   A                 T
A   R I C H A R D     V E N I C E     E
R   E L T     R       E       N       S
    W E   H   E R R O R S     A
      O   E   A   O   M       R
D   P   N   M   N   E             N
E   A   S       A       N O T H I N G
N   T       M           Y     G
M O O R     E   W I N D S O R     H E N R Y
A   A   T A L E           E     T
R       S   L
K       U   L
        R
  J U L I E T
```

157. AUTHORS OF POPULAR BOOKS FOR TEENS MAGIC SQUARE

A = 15	B = 6	C = 9	D = 4
E = 12	F = 1	G = 14	H = 7
I = 2	J = 11	K = 8	L = 13
M = 5	N = 16	O = 3	P = 10

158. AUTHORS OF POPULAR NOVELS FOR TEENAGERS CROSSWORD PUZZLE

```
 .  .  .  L  .  .  .  .  S  T  E  I  N  B  E  C  K  .  .  .  .  .  .
 S  P  E  R  R  Y  .  Z  .  A  .  .  .  O  .  O  .  L  E  E  .  .  .
 .  G  .  .  .  .  L  I  P  S  Y  T  E  N  .  R  .  O  .  .  B  .  .
 E  U  .  .  .  .  .  N  .  .  .  .  .  H  E  M  I  N  G  W  A  Y  .
 V  O  I  G  H  T  .  D  .  F  O  X  .  A  .  I  .  D  .  .  R  .  .
 E  N  I  .  .  .  .  E  .  R  .  .  .  M  .  E  .  O  .  .  R  .  G
 N  .  K  N  O  W  L  E  S  .  .  .  .  R  .  N  .  .  .  .  I  .  O
 S  .  .  T  .  H  .  .  .  .  .  D  .  .  K  .  .  O  D  E  L  L  L
 O  .  .  O  .  I  .  B  .  .  M  I  L  N  E  .  .  R  .  .  .  .  D
 N  .  .  N  .  T  W  A  I  N  .  C  .  .  Y  .  .  W  .  .  .  .  M
 .  .  .  E  .  U  .  .  .  .  .  K  G  E  O  R  G  E  .  .  .  .  A
 .  .  .  .  .  M  .  .  .  .  .  E  .  .  .  S  .  L  .  .  .  .  N
 .  .  .  .  .  U  .  .  .  .  .  N  .  .  .  .  .  L  .  .  .  .  .
 .  .  .  .  .  .  .  .  .  .  .  S  .  .  .  .  .  .  .  .  .  .  .
```

Across: 2 STEINBECK, 6 SPERRY, 8 LEE, 9 LIPSYTE, 11 HEMINGWAY, 12 VOIGHT, 14 FOX, 16 KNOWLES, 20 ODELL, 22 MILNE, 23 TWAIN, 24 GEORGE

159. FINDING THE TITLES OF FAMOUS LITERARY WORKS

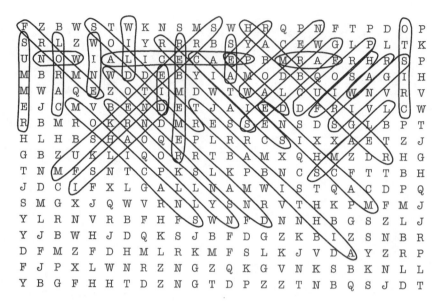

A Christmas <u>Carol</u>	Go Ask <u>Alice</u>
A Day No Pigs Would <u>Die</u>	I Know Why the Caged Bird <u>Sings</u>
A Night to <u>Remember</u>	Little <u>Women</u>
A Separate <u>Peace</u>	My Darling, My <u>Hamburger</u>
A Tale of Two <u>Cities</u>	One Fat <u>Summer</u>
A Tree Grows in <u>Brooklyn</u>	Rumble <u>Fish</u>
Alice's Adventures in <u>Wonderland</u>	Summer of My German <u>Soldier</u>
All Things Great and <u>Small</u>	That Was Then, This Is <u>Now</u>
Animal <u>Farm</u>	The Adventures of Tom <u>Sawyer</u>
Anne of Green <u>Gables</u>	The Chocolate <u>War</u>
Bridge to <u>Terabithia</u>	The Count of Monte <u>Cristo</u>
Call of the <u>Wild</u>	The Last of the <u>Mohicans</u>
Catcher in the <u>Rye</u>	The Old Man and the <u>Sea</u>
Dandelion <u>Wine</u>	The Three <u>Musketeers</u>
Death Be Not <u>Proud</u>	The Time <u>Machine</u>
Ethan <u>Frome</u>	Treasure <u>Island</u>

160. FAMOUS WOMEN AUTHORS

1. (D) Frank
2. (A) Austen
3. (B) Alcott
4. (B) Mitchell
5. (C) Hansberry
6. (C) Hurston
7. (A) Keller
8. (D) Wharton
9. (A) Porter
10. (A) Shelley

11. (D) Chopin
12. (A) Smith
13. (B) Eliot
14. (A) Dinesen
15. (C) Morrison
16. (C) Walker
17. (A) Woolf
18. (A) Lee
19. (D) Stowe
20. (B) Angelou

161. THINKING ABOUT BOOKS

Answers will vary.

162. ARE WE WHAT WE READ?

Answers will vary.

163. WHAT KIND OF READER ARE YOU?

Answers will vary.

164. A HERCULEAN TASK

```
         1M  A  2C  H  I  A  3V  E  4L  L  I  A  5N        6E
7B 8A B  B  L  E      A          E      I          E   9F  P  10B
 E  O          N      R          N      L  11P 12M A  R  T  I  A  L
 D  Y          T      D          U      L  E  S   E   C     O  O
 L  C          O      I          S      I  S  I   U  R     O
 A  O          R      G              P     T   I  D  E     M
 M  T          A              U     O  S   I      E       E
   13A T  L  A  S      N     14T I  T  A  N         A  N  R
    M                    A      I      I  15M      N  N  S
   16A D  O  N  I 17S      N      A     C  E
    Z              A       T      N        R
    O              T       A               C
    N              A       L               U
      18S I  R  E  N       I       19H E  R  M  E  T  I  C
                  I        Z               I
20P Y  R  R  H  I  C      21H E  R  C  U  L  E  A  N
                                           L
```

Across: 1 MACHIAVELLIAN · 7 BABBLE · 12 MARTIAL · 13 ATLAS · 14 TITAN · 16 ADONIS · 18 SIREN · 19 HERMETIC · 20 PYRRHIC · 21 HERCULEAN

165. REVIEW OF REAL AND FICTIONAL PEOPLE, PLACES, AND THINGS

A = 1	B = 10	C = 19	D = 23	E = 12
F = 18	G = 22	H = 11	I = 5	J = 9
K = 15	L = 4	M = 8	N = 17	O = 21
P = 7	Q = 16	R = 25	S = 14	T = 3
U = 24	V = 13	W = 2	X = 6	Y = 20

All columns and rows add up to 65.

166. DOCTOR, DOCTOR!

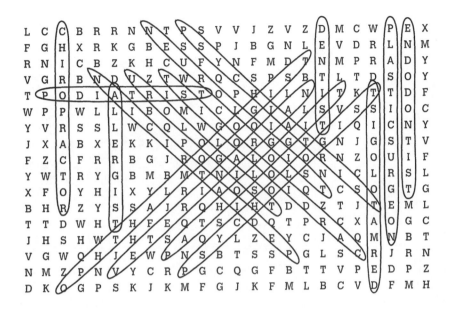

ALLERGIST	DERMATOLOGIST	PATHOLOGIST	PSYCHIATRIST
CARDIOLOGIST	ENDODONTIST	PEDIATRICIAN	PSYCHOLOGIST
CHIROPRACTOR	NEUROLOGIST	PLASTIC SURGEON	UROLOGIST
DENTIST	OPHTHALMOLOGIST	PODIATRIST	VETERINARIAN

167. EXPRESSIONS USING BODY PARTS

1. I	6. K	11. H	16. P
2. T	7. D	12. F	17. G
3. Q	8. S	13. A	18. N
4. E	9. L	14. J	19. C
5. B	10. M	15. O	20. R

168. FIRST NAMES AND BODY PARTS

169. CLICKING WITH CLICHÉS

A = 11	B = 13	C = 8	D = 2
E = 4	F = 6	G = 15	H = 9
I = 5	J = 3	K = 10	L = 16
M = 14	N = 12	O = 1	P = 7

170. WIN BROWNIE POINTS AND EARN ADVANCEMENT!

1. iw	11. ya
2. il	12. le
3. ln	13. xa
4. ot	14. nd
5. st	15. er
6. ea	16. th
7. la	17. eg
8. vi	18. re
9. ct	19. at
10. or	

"I will not steal a victory." Alexander the Great

171. AVOID THE CLICHÉS

1. a	8. e
2. v	9. c
3. o	10. l
4. i	11. i
5. d	12. c
6. t	13. h
7. h	14. e
	15. s

The message found in the answer column is, "Avoid the clichés."

172. DON'T GET CAUGHT BETWEEN A ROCK AND A HARD PLACE

1. shirt	6. egg	11. leg
2. boots	7. wall	12. eye
3. hats	8. closet	13. green
4. bacon	9. bed	14. red
5. pie	10. back	15. yellow

Common theme for 1–3 is things we wear.

Common theme for 4–6 is foods.

Common theme for 7–9 is things found in a room.

Common theme for 10–12 is body parts.

Common theme for 13–15 is colors.

173. THIS IS SUCH SWEET SORROW

1. g	6. n	11. o	16. q	21. b
2. m	7. t	12. d	17. u	
3. r	8. l	13. a	18. i	
4. k	9. h	14. j	19. p	
5. e	10. c	15. s	20. f	

The boy's name is Ken (4–6). The type of fish is cod (10–12). The witty remark is quip (16–19).

174. SHAKE A LEG AND POUR YOUR HEART OUT

1. t	6. i
2. h	7. n
3. r	8. t
4. o	9. h
5. w	10. e

The idiom (including its last word) is, "Throw in the towel."

175. EXPRESSIONS

1. Watch him
2. very annoying
3. pay close attention to
4. too hard to understand
5. clumsy
6. stay positive
7. do wrong
8. associate with
9. to become angry
10. nothing easy to do
11. what is not obviously presented
12. have an object of one's own to gain
13. unexpected winner
14. a difficult task
15. people of the same type

176. MORE EXPRESSIONS

1. the information is released
2. in a bad mood
3. spotless
4. no trace
5. do the same as everybody else (in a positive sense)
6. totally
7. close; hotly contested
8. come face to face with a difficult situation
9. anything he wants
10. in any way or method possible
11. faking it
12. gabbed; talked in a relaxed manner
13. considered precious
14. pay dearly
15. an accomplishment

177. PUTTING PROVERBS IN THEIR PROPER PLACES

Answers will vary. Discussion is encouraged.

178. WORDS THAT HAVE I AS THEIR SECOND LETTER

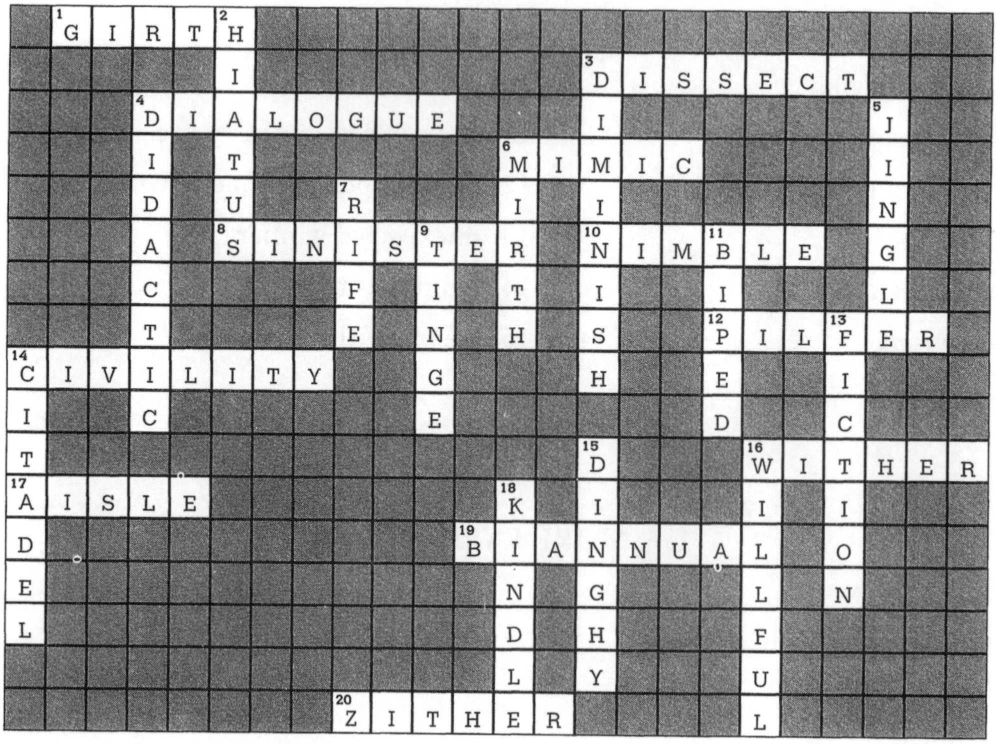

Crossword answer grid containing:

GIRTH, HITUACT (HITUACTT down), DISSECT, DIALOGUE, MIMIC, RITE, SINISTER, NIMBLE, PILFER, CIVILITY, WITHER, AISLE, BIANNUAL, ZITHER

Words/letters in grid:
- GIRTH
- DISSECT
- DIALOGUE
- MIMIC
- SINISTER — NIMBLE
- PILFER
- CIVILITY
- WITHER
- AISLE
- KINDLY
- BIANNUAL
- DIGHY
- ZITHER

Down entries: HITUACT..., DIDACT..., SFEINGE (RFEINGE), FITHNESH, MINISHED, WILLFUL, FICHE, CITADEL

179. TWO ON THE AISLE

Crossword answer grid containing:

- ACTOR
- SET
- PLOT
- COMEDY (C O U S...)
- ACOUSTICS
- AUDIENCE
- DRAMA
- STAGE
- USHER
- VILLAIN

Down entries: ACT, CONFLICT, COSTUME, SCENE, CHARACTER, DRAMATIST, MONOLOGUE, REHEARSAL, SUSPENSE, RIGHT

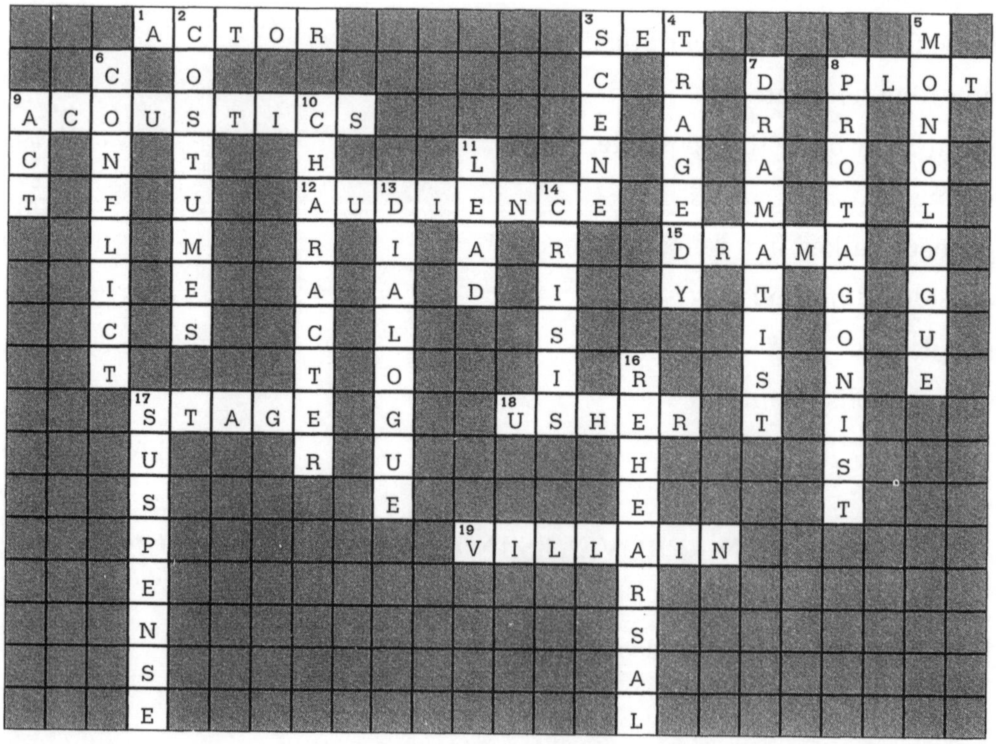

180. SOME FUN WITH WORDS

1. Teddy's steadies
2. Hale's tales
3. Stowe's woes
4. Ben's yens
5. Revere's ears
6. Turner's learners
7. George's forges
8. Hoover's louvers
9. Whitney's jitneys
10. Ford's cords
11. Harrison's garrisons
12. Keller's cellars
13. Long's wrongs
14. Welles' belles
15. Glenn's fens
16. Ride's rides
17. Souter's rooters
18. Ike's hikes
19. Martin's cartons
20. Bill's pills

181. ANIMALS IN THE LANGUAGE

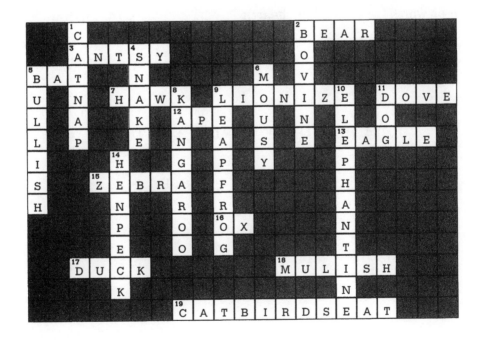

182. WHY DON'T YOU LOOK IN THE NEWSPAPER?

1. (b) Classifieds
2. (j) Travel
3. (e) Entertainment
4. (c) Comics
5. (h) Obituaries
6. (i) Sports
7. (d) Editorials
8. (a) Business
9. (f) Letters to the Editor
10. (g) News
11. (k) Weather

183. WHAT'S SO SPECIAL ABOUT NTH?

Possible answers are found below. There may be others.

1. path or pith
2. froth
3. broth or berth or birth
4. width or worth
5. dearth
6. stealth or seventh
7. breadth
8. wreath
9. hearth
10. uncouth
11. earth
12. smith
13. zenith
14. girth
15. mirth or month or mouth

184. HOW THESE WORDS CAME TO BE

1. P
2. E
3. R
4. H
5. N
6. B
7. G
8. J
9. I
10. T
11. C
12. A
13. Q
14. O
15. D
16. F
17. K
18. S
19. M
20. L

185. FOREIGN WORDS AND PHRASES

A = 7	B = 11	C = 6	D = 10
E = 14	F = 2	G = 15	H = 3
I = 12	J = 8	K = 9	L = 5
M = 1	N = 13	O = 4	P = 16

186. SPORTS HEADLINES

1. soar	6. conquer	11. sting	16. stampede
2. claw	7. cut	12. avoid	17. shatter
3. sink	8. scalp	13. baffle	18. outslick
4. rise	9. rustle	14. color	19. snare
5. arrest	10. roar	15. crown	20. burn